I0167453

A WHOLE NEW WAY TO WORK

A MAP TO FREEDOM AND SUCCESS

BRUCE ROBERT DOREY, PHD

LANGER BELL PRESS

Copyright © 2025 by Bruce Robert Dorey, PhD
Published by: Langer Bell Press

No part of this book may be reproduced in any form or by any electronic or mechanical
means, including information storage and retrieval systems, without written
permission from the author, except for the use of brief quotations in a book review.

All rights reserved.

ISBN: 979-8-218-66174-8

Printed in the USA.

To my father, thank you for instilling in me a love of engineering and science, for your endless curiosity, and for always encouraging me to explore new possibilities. Your passion for understanding how the world works has guided and shaped my own journey, influencing the way I think and create.

And to Vanessa, Alynn, Dani, and my dear friend Scotty—your love and support have been invaluable to me. Through every challenge and success, your belief in me has been my greatest strength. I am endlessly grateful to each of you.

With love and appreciation,

Bruce

CONTENTS

PREFACE

The Inspiration Behind the Book

I didn't write this book to introduce just another tech fad. I wrote it because, quite frankly, I needed to break free. For me, VR wasn't just a gadget—it was a lifeline, a gateway to a completely new way of living and working that pulled me out of a rut I didn't even know I was stuck in.

For years, I battled with focus, motivation, and the relentless pull of society's expectations—the pressure to fit into predetermined boxes, to follow well-trodden paths, and to measure success by someone else's rules. We're often handed this script early on: stick to the safe, the proven, and the familiar. But over time, those 'safe' paths become chains, suffocating you in the weight of routines and structures that promise security but deliver stagnation.

Then, I discovered VR. And it was like being hit with a jolt of clarity. It wasn't just different—it was a breakthrough. Suddenly, I wasn't following someone else's version of productivity or adhering to a timeline that wasn't mine. It felt like finally putting on glasses after years of squinting at a blurry world. I could see everything for what it was—clearly, without the fog of convention. For the first time, I could create my own space, set my own pace, and redefine what work meant to me. It wasn't just about getting more done; it was about feeling *alive.*

VR allowed me to design an environment that helped me find a deeper focus and immerse myself in the present. I could let go of all the rigid structures that had boxed me in for years. It was like hitting the reset button. The so-called 'right way' of doing things turned out to be nothing more than illusions holding me back. Once I broke free from that, I found an energy and confidence I didn't know I had. I realized I didn't need to follow the corporate blueprint, the old rules, or the safety nets of the past—I could forge my own path, and for the first time, I felt truly capable of thriving on my terms.

This book is my lifeline to you. It's a call to break free, reclaim your focus, and build a life where you set the rules. VR isn't just a tool; it's an invitation to rewrite your own story, to tear down the narratives that say you have to stay stuck in the same patterns. It's a chance to fully live in the present, unburdened by the past.

This book is more than just a guide; it's an invitation to take the controls and create your own adventure. It's about building a life where you don't just survive—you *thrive.* Work isn't about grinding through someone else's agenda but about living fully, growing, and finding joy in the journey. It's time to step into a new space, and VR is your gateway.

A Dynamic Approach to the End Notes and Appendix

As you read through this book, you may have noticed mentions of "end notes" or an appendix—these were placeholders for concepts, apps, or tools that I wanted to dive deeper into. But as I continued writing, I realized something: the pace of change in technology, especially in the world of VR and productivity, is relentless. Products evolve, new innovations pop up, and companies shift direction faster than you can test them.

So, rather than tying this book to static, and potentially outdated, information, I decided to create something dynamic—a living, breathing resource that evolves with you. I've built a website where you can access continually updated links to the latest products, tools, and ideas that align with the themes of this book. It's not just a repository; it's a curated hub that keeps pace with the ever-changing tech landscape.

By visiting www.BruceRDorey.com/WNWTW, you'll find the most up-to-date tools and innovations, tailored to help you on your journey toward productivity, focus, and living your best life. This way, you're not tied down by information that might already be out of date. Instead, you get a dynamic, evolving resource—one that grows and adapts just like the technology itself.

I want this resource to be more than just a website; I want it to be a bridge between you and the ongoing exploration of how we work, connect, and live. If you subscribe, you'll gain access to exclusive content, live webinars, and a community of like-minded individuals committed to harnessing the power of VR. Together, we'll stay at the forefront of the future of work, learning, and living. Dive in, explore, and discover how these tools can continue to transform your life—on your terms, at your pace.

INTRODUCTION

Amid the intricate sea of Wi-Fi waves, pixels, and flowing lines of code, we, engineers and creatives, stand at the threshold of the real and the virtual, crafting not just the world as it is, but as it could be. With silicon and steel, imagination and intellect, we shape the future, entrusted with the profound task of charting its course. This book offers a thoughtfully crafted foundation for your map—for those who have long sensed a better way to live and work that harmonizes with technology rather than resists it.

Neither digital abstinence nor blind submission will lead us forward; together, we can harness technology's potential to craft a harmonious space for living and working. But this journey isn't merely about building bridges or writing apps; it's about shifting our vision—about seeing the world not just as it is but as it could be.

Marcel Proust once wrote:

> "The real voyage of discovery consists not in seeking new land-scapes, but in having new eyes."

The true potential of AR and VR isn't rooted in their ability to create entirely new worlds, but in their power to transform how we perceive and engage with the world we already inhabit.

Proust's words remind us that the most profound shifts don't come from reaching distant horizons, but from viewing the familiar through a fresh lens. AR and VR serve as those lenses—revealing hidden connections, uncovering layers of possibility, and unlocking the untapped potential woven into the fabric of our current reality.

Before you dig into this book, I must be clear—this isn't about tweaking the status quo. There are no one-minute manager insights here. The map you'll find within these pages is for those of you who sense that their current, tradition-laden, and fear-driven existence is no way to live. It's for the visionaries who ask, *"Is this all there is?"* and refuse to accept that the map laid before them is the only option. But it's also a very practical guide, anchored in the real world.

While countless books delve into the 'why,' assuming we already know our purpose (I don't), this book answers the critical question of 'how'—how to get out of the swamp inside the wilderness we're born into and how to skip-step and flow through it in a way in which you flourish—in a world designed to keep you stuck in traffic, following some soulless script in an ocean of cubicles. It's for people like you who refuse to accept the status quo and instead seek to create a fulfilling and meaningful life.

Proust's *new eyes* philosophy is central to this exploration. VR, in particular, offers us a chance to re-envision our daily routines, our workplaces, and even our personal goals. It allows us to break free from the cycles that have kept us trapped in unfulfilling patterns, separated from the things we love, offering a fresh perspective that leads to genuine innovation and personal growth.

As engineers and creatives, you're near the front of the curve of this transformation. The technologies of AR and VR are not just new tools—they are gateways to new ways of thinking, working, and living in the same way as early printed books. They challenge us to move beyond the familiar, to explore the boundaries of our imagination, and to see our world with *new eyes*.

The future is not just something we enter; it is something we create. Let us, as McLuhan would say, understand the medium and, in doing so, shape the message for a future that aligns with our highest aspirations.

Many of us *jump* like lab rats to the visceral pangs of guilt when our paths don't conform to societal norms. But this way of living feels suffocating and unfulfilling. We may ask, "Is this all there is?" and question if there could be something better out there.

You've read the stories about how people wander in circles when lost in the wilderness without a map, convinced they're moving forward while paradoxically returning to where they started. I know this because I've walked those circular paths myself—armed with an illusory map based on formal education, societal expectations, and the deceptive security of 'certainty' in my direction. But each time, I found myself back at the beginning, anxious, depressed, depleted, and haunted by the relentless question, "Is this all there is?"

If you've ever felt that same nagging doubt, that sense of being trapped in an endless loop of unsatisfying progress, this book is for you. It's time to break free from the circles you're walking in and chart a new course—not one dictated by social media or consumer-driven distractions, but one that aligns with your goals and ambitions.

This book offers you the tools to do just that. Together, we'll navigate the complexities of the digital age, leveraging technology not as a crutch but as a catalyst for proper growth and fulfillment.

The journey begins now. Let's set the course.

Engineers, I truly admire your grit. The path you've chosen isn't just challenging because of the sheer complexity or volume of work—though grappling with differential equations or shadowboxing with quantum physics where certainty dissolves into probabilities would be enough to stop most. No, what makes your journey truly formidable is the relentless challenge of navigating this intellectual backcountry while resisting the siren call of safe paths.

You could have taken the guaranteed income of drilling, filling, and billing as a dentist or played it safe, managing the algorithms that manage some old guy's money, or, worse yet, wasted away trifurcating bond issues when a simple app that can and will do a better job. But you didn't. You chose engineering, driven by a deep-seated belief that you wanted to make something authentic and cool and, oh yeah, to get to a flow state doing it. You believed that the laws of science would guide you toward your dreams—dreams of creating, innovating, and maybe even, like Elon, Richard, or Jeff - reaching for the stars.

As you embark on this journey, think about the humble beginnings of giants like Sir Isaac Newton, who once lectured to rooms so empty they'd get zero likes on social media. His persistence in the face of utter obscurity is a testament to what resilience and unwavering belief in one's vision can accomplish and the legacy it can leave.

So, what will your legacy be? How will your contributions refine the map of human progress? This book—my second—is a tribute to you, the engineer and creative professional brave enough to embrace the new frontier of AR and VR technology. It's an invitation to use these incredible tools as guiding stars, leading us through uncharted territories to horizons we've only dreamed of.

Look back at history—each pivotal moment, from the printing press to the steam engine, the discovery of electricity to the internal combustion engine, the digital revolution, and, of course, AI —every one of these breakthroughs didn't just change the world; they redrew the map of *how*. They shaped where, when, and how we work and live, often in ways we never anticipated.

Now, we're at the edge of another seismic shift—the era of augmented and virtual reality. These aren't just cool gadgets or the next tech fad; they are profound extensions of our reality, not replacements. AR and VR are the new fabric or material of creation, the new languages of innovation, adding layers of depth and possibility to our world that we're only beginning to explore.

Like a shimmering lens, AR overlays our physical world with digital layers, like fortnight *gold bars* appearing on a map.

Conversely, VR rips open the fabric of our reality entirely, inviting us into new worlds—truly virgin territory where your imagination reigns supreme. It's the Marauder's Map, revealing every secret passage in Hogwarts. With VR, you can scale the sheer rock face of El Cap, work alongside Carl Jung in Bollingen Tower, on Lake Zurich, or orbit the earth.

VR is more than just a cool gadget; it's also a gym for your brain. It is resistance training for cognition, toning your focus, and pumping up your capacity to think and learn.

AR and VR are more than technological advancements—they are the new human renaissance. Just like Ptolemy and Captain Cook redefined the world with their maps, you can redefine the human experience using AR and VR. They challenge us to look beyond the physical, reimagine our world, and see beyond the wilderness to a future ripe for exploration.

And while we've come a long way, the truth is simple but profound: the technologies we've embraced in the past haven't just shaped us—they've confined us. What we once hailed as revolutionary has become tools or, better still, cudgels for wealthy corporations and governments to control our actions, limit our freedoms, and trap us in outdated, inefficient systems - burning "our" (not their) precious earth resources. We're moving through a world cluttered with the waste products of these old ways, weighed down by institutional "bullshit."

But there's a way out. AR and VR aren't just new technologies but the keys to a more liberated, meaningful life. Unlike their predecessors, AR and VR don't trap us—they free us.

They break down the barriers of space and time, allowing us to experience the world in new and immersive ways. And as we immerse ourselves in these virtual worlds, we begin to see our physical world with fresh eyes.

Richard Feynman put it perfectly:

> "When we look at a flower, what we're seeing is only a tiny part of the electromagnetic spectrum. All kinds of other waves, like radio waves and X-rays, pass through us, but our eyes are tuned to a very narrow band. Amazingly, when we look out, we don't see a sea of waves, a tumult of energy. The world is so much richer than what we perceive with our senses."[1]

As engineers, you're at the crossroads of science and magic, with the power to create wonders that were unimaginable just a generation ago.

Arthur C. Clarke nailed it when he said:

> *"Any sufficiently advanced technology is indistinguishable from magic."*

This book is your guide to navigating the magical, uncharted world of AR and VR. It's here to help you find your place in this new world and use these tools to shape your life and the world around you.

Why write this book now? In the twilight of my years, I've often wondered, "Is this all there is?" The answer, I've realized, lies within me and the extraordinary journey I've been privileged to experience. This book is the culmination of that journey, a map for my future and yours.

So, as you read on, think about your path and the one that lies ahead. Consider the roads you've walked over and over and those still waiting to be explored. Where will it take you? The answer isn't just in these pages—it's within you.

THE DAWN OF A NEW ERA IN SALES ENGINEERING

Virtual Morning Routine

Routines, the guiding stars that illuminate our path through the labyrinth of existence, offer solace and direction amidst the tumultuous currents of modernity. In the symphony of chaos, routines stand as the conductor, orchestrating the dance of discipline and resilience. With each practiced ritual, we carve a path toward our aspirations, sculpting our destinies with unwavering determination. These sacred rituals, akin to the ancient rites of passage, bestow upon us a mantle of empowerment, allowing us to navigate the ebb and flow of time with grace and fortitude. As we honor the rhythm of our routines, we unlock the boundless potential that lies dormant within our souls.

In a world where technology seamlessly intertwines with daily life, sales engineers like myself start each day with a distinctively innovative approach. My morning begins not with the shrill of an alarm but with the soothing sound of ocean waves that signal the start of my virtual bike ride. I slip on my VR headset, connect it to my advanced haptic bike, and find myself transported to a picturesque oceanfront. Here, the bike mimics every tilt and turn of the terrain, making my exercise not just a routine but an exhilarating experience that awakens both body and mind.

I first took up the morning ritual of riding bikes more than 20 years ago. The cool morning air danced on my skin, invigorating my senses and igniting a fervor for life's endless possibilities. In the serene backdrop of nature's symphony, I found solace and serenity that liberated me from the confines of the mundane and transported me to a realm of boundless freedom. With each mile conquered and obstacle overcome, the morning ride became a form of exercise and a sacred pilgrimage toward physical and emotional well-being.

Today, I can go on that very same pilgrimage in the comfort of my own home. Beside me, my personal AI coach, resembling my best friend, pushes me through a challenging 30-minute interval ride. We strive to hit our target heart rates, a vital part of our weekly fitness goals. This immersive experience[1], complete with the 360-degree view and the lifelike sounds of seagulls and waves, sets a perfect tone for another productive day.

Seamless Transition to Work

Traveling through congested streets and highways, stuck in endless traffic jams, is nothing short of a soul-crushing experience. The constant stop-and-go, the blaring horns, and the fumes from exhaust pipes make every journey a tedious ordeal. What should be a simple trip from point A to point B turns into a frustrating battle against time and circumstance. Hours wasted in traffic feel like a theft of precious moments that could have been better spent on more meaningful pursuits. The dullness of the commute drains that early morning energy and enthusiasm, leaving behind an overwhelming sense of irritation and discontent.

Transitioning from my bike ride to work used to take me hours. Nowadays, after a rejuvenating shower and a cup of my favorite coffee, I just step into my home study, where I gear up for the weekly company-wide project review meeting.

This efficiency has transformed my mornings from a cumbersome ordeal into a seamless transition, allowing me to reclaim valuable time that was once lost to the tediousness of travel and preparation. Freed from the shackles of traffic congestion and the constraints of physical distance, I now find myself instantly immersed in the rhythm of productivity, ready to tackle the day's challenges with renewed vigor and clarity of purpose.

The reduction in commuting has enhanced my well-being and contributed positively to the environment. Fewer vehicles on the road mean lower emissions, less pollution, and a smaller carbon footprint. This shift towards remote work represents a collective step towards sustainability, highlighting how individual lifestyle changes can have a broader impact on the planet. As we adapt to this new normal, it becomes increasingly evident that the benefits extend beyond personal convenience, fostering a more sustainable and harmonious way of living.

Transformative Meeting Experience

Traditional meetings, with their stifling confines and labyrinthine agendas, often resemble a descent into the depths of bureaucratic purgatory. The monotony of endless discussions, punctuated by the drone of one uninspired PowerPoint presentation after another and the incessant ticking of the clock, transforms each gathering into a torturous ordeal. Attendees, shackled by the chains of formality and protocol, find themselves trapped in a cycle of inefficiency and frustration as the inertia of tradition stifles innovation and progress.

The hierarchical structure of traditional meetings breeds a culture of conformity, where dissenting voices are silenced, and creativity is quashed beneath the weight of conformity and general discomfort. With every minute that passes, the soul-sucking ennui of the conference room engulfs participants, draining their energy and enthusiasm until all that remains is a hollow shell of apathy and resignation.

Gone are the days of gathering our large sales team in one physical location. Now, our meetings unfold in the digital realm, bridging the geographical divides that once hindered collaboration. Through the marvels of technology, we convene virtually, transcending the limitations of time and space. No longer constrained by the logistical burdens of travel, our discussions flow effortlessly, unencumbered by the distractions of physical proximity.

In the virtual meeting room, I find myself in my preferred spot, center room, two rows back. The remarkable aspect is that everyone gets their preferred spot, independent of physical space limitations. This is a very different experience from that of Zoom or Teams, where pixelated faces and stilted interactions often resemble a digital purgatory devoid of life and vitality. The sterile confines of the virtual conference room, bereft of the warmth and camaraderie of face-to-face interaction, amplify the sense of isolation and disconnection.

Those unfortunate enough to be part of those meetings, reduced to mere squares on a screen, struggle to convey emotion and nuance through the cold medium of technology. The constant interruptions of lagging audio and frozen screens disrupt the flow of conversation, creating an atmosphere of frustration and discord. As the hours drag on, the monotony of the meeting becomes a relentless assault on the senses, draining energy and enthusiasm with each passing minute. Despite the best efforts of participants to engage and connect, the lifeless void of this simplistic virtual realm renders the experience a pale imitation of its real-world counterpart and the superior AR/VR-assisted experience.

Through his avatar, the meeting leader seems to speak directly to me, tracking my eye movement and ensuring a personal connection despite the digital setting. Our interactions are more than just avatars nodding; they're a fusion of human empathy and technological sophistication.

In these meetings, we focus on rapid, effective information sharing. We've learned that the key isn't just housing data in complex software; it's about creating a system that works intuitively with the engineer. This approach is informed by cutting-edge research, including insights from Stanford's AR-VR Lab, emphasizing that the synergy between human intelligence and technological aid far exceeds the use of either alone or without the symbiosis.

Our project tracking and updates are the backbone of these meetings. The aim is to circulate relevant information among those who can add value through experience or personal connections. This isn't just another meeting to endure; it's a wellspring of useful information, aiding both our personal growth and business objectives.

Unique Features of the Meeting

The incorporation of avatars not only introduces a lifelike dimension but also underscores the transformative nature of our meetings. Unlike traditional meetings that often stretch over 3-5 tedious hours, our current affairs are now condensed into two concise 45-minute sessions. In contrast to the constraints of physical and Zoom meetings, where document sharing and updates were cumbersome and time-consuming, I can seamlessly access and distribute vital information during my presentation. Orders, acknowledgments, shipping, and everything else I need are floating in my virtual space and curated by my real or virtual assistants. Integrating APIs, real-time shipping updates, and live video feeds from job sites further enhances our operational efficiency, significantly departing from conventional meetings' logistical hurdles.

Behind-the-Scenes Team

While my avatar represents me in the meeting, a dedicated team works tirelessly behind the scenes. Assistants, estimators, and logistics coordinators all play crucial roles, ensuring that the virtual representation is just the tip of the iceberg.

As I delve into my projects, highlighting their impact on our quarterly metrics, it becomes clear that this technological revolution isn't just about efficiency; it's about changing the very nature of our work.

Beyond Work: A Social and Personal Revolution

Like every previous era, there's criticism about this tech-driven approach's seemingly 'non-social' nature. I, however, advocate for the profound benefits this technology brings. In embracing this digital revolution, we liberate ourselves from the shackles of mundane existence. We reclaim precious moments previously squandered in the chaos of traffic, parking dilemmas, and endless queues.

The advent of tools like the Rize[2] app heralds a paradigm shift, offering efficient scheduling solutions and invaluable insights into our daily routines. No longer beholden to the confines of a fixed office space or rigid work hours, we are empowered to craft a lifestyle that fits our individual needs and rhythms, fostering both productivity and personal satisfaction.

Drawing inspiration from the transformative evolution of dating apps, we witness a seismic shift in the dynamics of human connection. Where once physical appearance reigned supreme, the spotlight now shines on shared interests and values, facilitating more profound and meaningful connections. With the emergence of augmented reality (AR) and virtual reality (VR) apps, we transcend the limitations of physical boundaries, forging bonds untainted by biases and prejudices.

This technological inflection point transcends mere shifts in work habits; it marks a profound leveling of the social landscape, ushering in an era defined by honesty, efficiency, and fulfillment. As we embark on this journey of exploration, we peel back the layers of this profound transformation, delving into its myriad implications for our collective well-being and societal fabric. In the following chapter, we will navigate the intricacies of this digital revolution, illuminating the path toward a brighter, more interconnected future.

Reimagining our daily lives through technology is more than a convenience; it's a movement towards a society where time is no longer a commodity to be managed but a resource to be cherished. This newfound freedom allows us to invest in our passions, strengthen our relationships, and cultivate a deeper connection with ourselves and the world around us. By leveraging the power of these technological advancements, we can achieve a balance between work and personal life that was once thought impossible.

As we continue to explore the possibilities and embrace the changes brought forth by this digital age, it is crucial to remain mindful of the potential pitfalls. While technology can undoubtedly enhance our lives, it is up to us to ensure that it does not overshadow the human element central to our existence. By striking a harmonious balance, we can harness the full potential of this revolution, creating a future where technology and humanity coexist and thrive together.

2

THE MAPS WE ARE GIVEN

The opening chapter began our journey by giving you a glimpse at the destination. This isn't just a physical place but a realm of intentional living. It's a lifestyle choice that, when embraced, unfolds the most enriching and satisfying existence conceivable.

While I am not an advocate of spending the day on a couch with a headset, my ultimate message is that by working in this new way, you'll do more and better work in shorter periods, giving you more time and opportunity to do the things you love, with the people you love, in the places you love.

Misalignment with Modern Needs

Traditional office environments and rigid schedules fail to accommodate the diverse needs of today's workforce. Flexible and adaptive work environments, such as those enabled by VR and AR technologies, have boosted productivity and job satisfaction by providing personalized workspaces and schedules.

Breaking Free from the Norms

We can create spaces conducive to deep work and personal satisfaction by embracing new technologies and rethinking our work environments. This transformation is akin to the revolutionary impact of air conditioning on productivity and comfort. Just as we wouldn't accept sweltering workplaces, we shouldn't settle for inefficient and outdated work practices.

To reveal a whole new way to work, we need to shovel away some of the Bullshit, starting with the notion that "who am I to question conforming to this existing rigid, oppressive structure and environment.

The 1984 Apple Super Bowl commercial, directed by Ridley Scott, profoundly impacted me and millions of others; the feeling it elicited still resonates with me today. Scott was already renowned for directing *Blade Runner*, a film of Philip K. Dick's dystopian novel *Do Androids Dream of Electric Sheep?* where Harrison Ford portrayed Rick Deckard, a "blade runner" hunting down renegade human replicants. A few years later, Scott directed Apple's iconic 1984 Super Bowl commercial.

This ad depicted a bleak, monotonous, and repressive work environment, which was dramatically disrupted by the introduction of Apple's Macintosh, symbolizing a revolution that freed individuals from the chains of the past-based Bullshit.

Initially embraced with optimism, the fight against uniformity began to wane in the 80s and 90s, succumbing to political conservatism and a corporate focus on profits. Despite this, the seeds of rebellion sown by that daring Super Bowl ad continued to grow, slowly preparing future generations to resist conformity.

Today, it's clear that we must let go of outdated Bullshit and oppressive work rituals and embrace a whole new way of working. Inspired by the pioneering spirit of *Blade Runner* and the Apple commercial, we can break free from the rigid norms of the past and forge a path toward a healthier, creative, and fulfilling work environment. Today, with the benefit of Moores's Law, we stand at the precipice of change.

Welcome to a Whole New World of Work

Many people accept the status quo, believing "it is ain't broke, don't fix it," and, due to cultural momentum, fear of change and established networks are the only viable options. However, data on personal performance, mental health, and job satisfaction tell a different story. It turns out that the current system might indeed be broken.

The common perception is that VR is a tool for escaping reality. Detractors insist they're pushing us away from the "real" world and the essential human experiences we hold dear, such as empathy, love, and appreciation of beauty. To this, I firmly say that's total crap (not the same as Bullshit, mind you).

I don't use the words "crap" or "bullshit" without some deliberation. The term "crap" has a history relevant to the central theme of the book, both in terms of its etymology and its evolution to signify something of low quality or worthlessness, such as useless information.

Contrary to popular belief, the word is not directly derived from Thomas Crapper, the 19th-century British plumber who popularized the flush toilet. This connection is more folklore than factual.

The true origin of "crap" can be traced back to the Middle English "crappie," which referred to chaff or discarded husks of grain and is likely derived from the Medieval Latin "crappie," meaning chaff. Initially, the term was related to agricultural waste or byproducts, which were often discarded and had little to no value. This concept of discarding worthless material likely influenced its later usage.

By the early 20th century, "crap" became more commonly associated with feces, further solidifying its connotation as something undesirable or worthless. The transition to describing anything generally useless or of poor quality followed naturally from these associations. The term's evolution reflects a typical pattern in language where words associated with waste and refuse gain broader metaphorical meanings that encompass notions of poor quality, uselessness, or something contemptible.

So, just as "crap" was historically something to be discarded, I suggest that outdated work practices should be recognized as "Crap" and removed from modern workflows.

"Bullshit," however, carries a very different and more specific connotation. The term gained significant traction in modern discourse partly due to philosopher Harry Frankfurt's exploration in his essay "On Bullshit." Frankfurt describes "bullshit" as statements made without regard to truth, more about the speaker's intention to persuade or impress than adherence to factual accuracy. This definition has made "bullshit" particularly suited to describing practices that are not just ineffective but are perceived as deliberately deceptive or constructed to maintain appearances rather than achieve substantive results.

But it was David Graeber, a PhD from the University of Chicago, who, while teaching at Yale and the London School of Economics, wrote a book on this very distinction which is most closely associated with my experience, called "Bullshit Jobs." Here, he dives deeply into the phenomenon in which many jobs in modern society are considered pointless, meaningless, or unnecessary. The central thesis of his book is that many people find themselves trapped in "bullshit jobs" that provide little personal satisfaction or societal benefit. But because of our status quo bias, which includes the aversion to uncertainty and loss, we stay in what we call "secure" jobs.

These jobs, even labeled executives-level jobs, offer no opportunity for personal mastery or autonomy and, worse, no experience in contributing to anything meaningful. Despite this, employees are continuously trained and expected to appear busy and productive, leading to existential despair and an ever-increasing reliance on SSRIs (anti-depression drugs).

In contexts like corporate environments, government, or other large organizations, "bullshit" can also effectively encapsulate the frustration of red tape, bureaucratic inertia, and practices that serve more to obfuscate or complicate rather than to streamline or enlighten. It suggests disregarding genuine efficiency or transparency, focusing instead on maintaining a façade or fulfilling arbitrary procedural requirements.

I digress. There are still those in positions of some power who will try to make you believe that inhaling fumes in a metal and polyethylene box on the massive smoggy pavement is the definition of "The Real World." Or the actual experience of life is found crammed in a subway car, surrounded by people leached of dignity and energy by the dullness of commuting, not to mention a Petre dish of viruses capable of taking you out of the game for two weeks. While trying to authentically illuminate this essence, I'm reminded that my most recent real-world experience is a cubicle-bound existence with no objective view of anything other than more cubicle-bound office buildings.

Again I digress, Bullshit does that (digress) to the best of us, but I promise to share with you the map to a whole new way of working, which will keep you from a day full of digression.

We're about to embark on a journey to fulfillment, starting at work in the real or objective "measurable real" world, which includes all technologies, including VR. The MAP to be created for you is clearly marked to lead you there. For the skeptics among us, allow me to tell you a painful yet personal story that underscores my commitment to the transformative power of VR technology.

Ready Player One

The end of my marriage was an awful experience that reshaped my entire outlook on life. When I met and fell deeply in love with my soon-to-be ex-wife, we were involved in "so-called" self-help transformation seminars. As new residents of Houston with no family or friends, these seminars became an integral part of our lives, blurring the lines between our marriage and the relentless cycle of self-improvement sessions.

I was swept up in the crowd contagion, strategically elicited to drive more sales, and naively believed this would sustain our marriage and provide an exciting new way of life. Conforming to these rituals was meant to motivate us to feel good and, therefore, sell more seminars, but they did not address the challenges of marriage. The profound disappointment I feel from conforming to these empty rituals has taught me the importance of breaking away from such ineffective practices and seeking a whole new way to work and live. This way genuinely supports and nourishes our true selves and relationships.

After standing in the crowded, depressing Houston courthouse and finalizing the divorce papers, I stepped into the even more oppressive Houston summer heat, feeling neither joy nor sorrow. I sought relief —from the institution of marriage, the routines, habits, and the facade it was. I thought she was the problem and ending the marriage would solve everything. But I realized the life I was fleeing was constructed from my past-based beliefs and society's imposed goals, dreams, and consumables.

This started a period of profound introspection and adjustment, during which I questioned my past decisions and beliefs about my future.

My marriage did not end like every Disney movie I had watched growing up, which I assumed would be afforded to me. But the reality for both of us was that we were "failures." And now, I was faced with the daunting task of starting over.

Marriage is an institutional practice followed by millions, only to have roughly half of those who accepted the ritual be left somewhat broken or diminished after the fact. When I think about the pain I felt and the pain I must have inflicted on someone whom I once deeply loved, I realize that for me and many others, this institutional practice of marriage in your 20s is crap. I say this because of the data: since the 1970s, the marriage rate in the US has plummeted by nearly 60%. In 1970, it was 76.5%, but now it's around 31.1%. At the same time, divorce rates surged, particularly in the 1980s.

Look, the truth is I didn't dig into what was important as a way to prepare for marriage, like talking about our shared beliefs, dreams, hopes, and aspirations. Honestly, my marriage and wife-to-be merely fit the picture, perfectly rendered for the story in my head.

Finding Connection in a Virtual World

After my divorce, I felt trapped in a relentless cycle of sadness and regret that eroded my self-esteem and confidence. I had just moved to Pennsylvania alone and only knew a few people. Typically, I would call my Mom, and somehow she would make me feel better, but since her death a year earlier, this too was a painful thought. One particularly gloomy Sunday morning, I dreaded the thought of Monday and returning to a job I didn't love. But it was still 10 a.m., and I could cozy up on the couch, burn time, and escape my fear of dating again. I watched some TV but found solace and adventure in online forums, particularly relating to classic rock. When I was online, I was engaged and less likely to slip into anxiety and depression.

In 1999, VR was still clunky, but online forums like Harmony Central[1] were popular for connecting with others. This new technology offered a safe and autonomous way to meet and discuss interests, primarily classic rock, without fear of judgment or heartbreak.

On Harmony Central, I found a community of what appeared to be "normal people" and met someone unexpected—a fellow engineer who shared my passion for politics and the band Rush. Engaging in pseudo-intellectual conversations about Rush's drummer Neil Peart's "objectivist" lyrics felt avant-garde, and it was strangely enlivening. Our cautious yet exhilarating interactions revealed layers of our personalities that felt more genuine than anything I had experienced in years.

We listened to music and shared thoughts on everything from politics (she worked as a consultant for the Obama administration) to the connections between Rush's music, Nathaniel Brandon, and Frank Herbert's writing. I learned genuine connection isn't about physical proximity, looks, or race. It's about finding someone who understands and accepts you for who you are beyond society's labels and expectations.

I found the courage to redefine love on my terms through this online technology. It wasn't about conforming to status or chasing fleeting moments of sexual ecstasy; it was about building a friendship and companionship based on mutual interests, shared values, and a genuine desire to grow together—and yes, a love of the music of Rush and Led Zeppelin.

By embracing technology, she and I discovered a love transcending traditional relationships. Our bond flourished in the virtual realm and eventually extended into the "real" world, where we occasionally traveled together for a brief get-a-way or just emailed, even while living on opposite coasts of the United States. However, my move to Paris in 2000 proved too great a distance for our relationship.

Looking back, I understand timelines or societal expectations don't bind that true love. It's a profoundly personal journey of self-discovery and acceptance that online technology helped me navigate with newfound clarity and optimism.

Much like the world depicted in *Ready Player One*, where Wade Watts (Parzival) and Samantha Cook (Art3mis) find genuine connection and purpose in The Oasis and Columbus, Ohio, my experience showed me that love and authenticity can flourish in both the real and virtual worlds. I envision a future where love is defined by authenticity, connection, and the courage to embrace new possibilities, whether real or virtual.

I'm not merely painting a positive picture of technology as the way to a brighter future because I know that is not true now, as it was not the case 100 years ago at the beginning of the technology revolution.

I am making the case that VR technology is an extraordinary breakthrough. When used wisely and judiciously, it will provide you with an objectively more successful and satisfying work experience.

Imagine if, in the early days of the telephone, someone had suggested it would be used not just for personal messaging but for negotiating all forms of business deals and coordinating complex projects across the globe. People would have been skeptical that technology could replace the good old face-to-face communication, yet today, we can't imagine a world without it. Just as the telephone revolutionized communication by making it instantaneous and accessible, VR is transforming our interactions and work habits in digital environments.

Today, more individuals spend time and money in these digital spaces than at all forms of movies and sporting events combined. This surge of interest isn't a mere techno trend; there's genuine merit to it, which words alone on a page can hardly convey. If you're yet to explore the world of VR, I recommend that you get started immediately. You could pop into one of the major retail stores for a demo or order a Quest 2 or 3 headset, or if money is not a limiting factor, buy the Apple Vision Pro for about 8-9 X the price.

What you'll discover, like millions worldwide, is the overwhelming engagement that the VR environment can create. It is captivating and visually delightful; it's remarkable. To begin your journey, spend some quality time exploring VR. Getting used to it is essential to fully understanding and appreciating this book's recommendations. A great starting point would be to utilize the free version of the "Immersed"[2] app by Meta. It's an easy first step into the world of VR. Detail instructions are found in the Appendix, but frankly, I suggest using an AI like Chat GPT, to help you learn how to use it.

But there's no better way to learn VR than by diving right into it. As you familiarize yourself, you'll understand how to replicate your desktop. The brilliance here is that you can sit in any one of a few spectacular locations and pull up your desktop. The key is to leap and "just do it." Stop procrastinating. Once you get past this initial learning curb, designing your day in VR will start making much more sense.

The end of a marriage is a transformative event that reshapes every aspect of one's life, a truth I came to understand all too well. As the final papers were signed and the reality of my situation sank in, I stood at the threshold of a new, unfamiliar world. The life I had known, built on shared dreams and promises, had crumbled away, leaving me to navigate the debris of a broken heart and the daunting task of rebuilding my identity as a single individual. It was a time of profound introspection and adjustment, filled with questions about the future and how I would fit into this new narrative I had never anticipated.

Navigating through the aftermath, I encountered the universal agony that erodes self-esteem and confidence over time. The thought of reentering the dating scene felt like a daunting, heart-racing endeavor I was reluctant to embark upon. During a period marked by depression and vulnerability, I found solace in front of the television, a piece of technology that, unbeknownst to me, would play a pivotal role in my healing. Working in New York City, thanks to my affinity for maps and the quaint charm of old bookshops, I stumbled on a connection to "The Shop Around the Corner," a fictional bookstore from the movie *You've Got Mail*. This store, epitomizing the essence of traditional bookstores as hubs for genuine connection through literature, resonated deeply with me.

The story of Kathleen Kelly and Joe Fox, battling the encroachment of a corporate giant while unknowingly finding companionship through anonymous emails, highlighted the dichotomy between personal touch and corporate efficiency. This story, paralleling my life, illustrated how technology, even as simple as email, can bridge divides, fostering authentic connections beyond societal barriers.

This experience illuminated the current potential of Augmented Reality (AR) and Virtual Reality (VR) technologies. Much like the email exchanges between Kathleen and Joe, AR and VR can transcend physical and social limitations, offering immersive experiences that foster deeper connections regardless of geographical or societal divides. These technologies promise a more equitable playing field, challenging the biases tied to physical attributes and enabling a meritocracy where the best ideas prevail, irrespective of the creator's background.

My time in the Middle East exposed the stark realities of discrimination based on race, gender, and nationality. White individuals from North America or Europe were treated with a level of respect not afforded to those from Africa or South Asia. This stark bias exposed the untapped reservoirs of creativity and intelligence stifled by these prejudices. VR offers hope, capable of breaking down these barriers and fostering a more inclusive and diverse environment for problem-solving and innovation. AR and VR are beacons of hope, capable of dismantling these barriers and facilitating a more inclusive and diverse approach to problem-solving and innovation.

Drawing parallels between my journey through the dating world and professional advancements in engineering design, it's evident that technology has the power to level the playing field across various aspects of life. From virtual meetings that circumvent unconscious biases to democratizing creativity in engineering, technology offers a glimpse into a future where barriers continuously crumble.

Reflecting on the numerous collaborative projects that stretched across continents, the transformative impact of Augmented Reality (AR) and Virtual Reality (VR) becomes evident in their capacity to dismantle traditional boundaries of location and environment. These technologies are redefining how we forge connections, offering more than just digital interactions; they facilitate a shared virtual space where ideas can converge and evolve in real-time. This is particularly revolutionary in fields like engineering, where VR allows for the creation and manipulation of virtual prototypes. These virtual models are not merely static images but interactive entities that teams across the globe can work on simultaneously. This capability enables immediate feedback and iterative design processes without geographical limitations.

The speed at which these innovations can be developed, tested, and refined is unprecedented. By reducing the time from concept to market, VR and AR enhance productivity and foster a culture of rapid innovation. This shift is crucial for staying competitive in today's fast-paced global economy. The integration of diverse perspectives is not an afterthought but a foundational aspect of the design process. This inclusivity is essential for creating solutions that are truly global and resonate with a broad audience. The ability to collaborate in real-time with team members from different cultural and professional backgrounds enriches the development process, leading to more holistic and innovative outcomes. This new paradigm of collaborative problem-solving, powered by AR and VR, promises to reshape industries and redefine what it means to work together.

This intertwining of technology in both personal and professional spheres provides a hopeful outlook on a future where inclusivity and equity are paramount. As we delve deeper into the capabilities of AR and VR, we'll explore their impact on industries, education, and personal expression. Through stories, case studies, and pragmatic arguments, I aim to unveil the limitless possibilities at the intersection of technology and humanity, charting a course through this new, leveled landscape—a map guiding us to a future where every individual has the opportunity to flourish.

3

WHEN THE RUSH REPLACES DREAMS

Breaking Free from the Chains of the Daily Grind

One morning, as I sped through traffic, barely noticing that the coffee was burning my tongue, it hit me: this crazy new routine, the powerful adrenaline rush, was slowly replacing my dreams. I didn't give them up in some grand USS Missouri moment of defeat—I let them slip away, piece by piece, trading my deeply held aspirations for the daily grind. In the MEP industry, where chaos is the norm, it's easy to fall into this trap. You convince yourself that the relentless demands of the day justify abandoning your bigger goals. But the truth is brutal: those routines you lean on aren't just habits but chains. Chains that bind you to a version of yourself that has quietly surrendered what truly matters.

I've seen it everywhere—from boardrooms where decisions are driven by fear of change and political posturing to CAD stations where creativity is stifled by the fear of pissing off "manufacturing." These habits have taken root so deeply that they've convinced you this is just the way it is. But is it? Or have you accepted that this is all there ever will be?

The MEP industry, however, doesn't thrive on routine or the predictability of a 9-to-5—it runs on the wild oscillations of dealing with clients, contractors, manufacturers, and the constant flux of technology. Each day is a race against time, a high-stakes engineering challenge where you're constantly troubleshooting and problem-solving. There is big money at stake, with sales over a million dollars a year. Every hour brings a new fire to put out, a new obstacle to overcome.

This race is addicting, but it's one in which you are always behind and just barely catching up. On a good day, with almost no effort, you're swept up on the adrenaline express, and after a day of furious activity, you get back to zero—having held your ground but making no progress.

What if I told you there's a new way to approach this chaos? VR offers a map that can turn these constant challenges into opportunities for streamlined efficiency. Join me in exploring this new reality, and let's discover how we can transform the turbulence of the MEP world into a precisely engineered process of order and innovation.

This is your moment to stop surviving and start thriving. To stop making excuses and start making progress. I have found that "The Truth will set you free," and for many of us, the truth is we put up with a lot of Bullshit because of fear and, what is worse, we don't think the real you is enough to fulfill your dreams.

The Adrenaline Rush

Patrick Lencioni's book *The Advantage*[1] beautifully captures the essence of the adrenaline rush. I found myself addicted to this surge of energy because it infused my days with a sense of self-importance and short-term purpose. Each day was a battle to wrestle order from chaos, and there was a strange satisfaction in that struggle. This cycle of chaos and control was familiar to me through personal experience, and as the legacy I saw in my father's footsteps. It provided a semblance of certainty and challenge, a path well-trodden by those before us.

However, reflecting on how much this reactive lifestyle controls and limits us reveals more profound insights into what truly makes a life well-lived. It pushes us to question the rituals and habits that drive us and to confront the quiet doubts whispering, "Is this all there is?"

This reflection has challenged me to break free from the confines of our routines and seek a more fulfilling and intentional way of living.

The core of this book isn't just about expanding your horizons; it's about challenging the way you think about work. It's a push to question outdated routines and find the courage to break free from traditional constraints. This book offers a clear, actionable plan and a roadmap to explore a broader range of possibilities. VR shouldn't be seen as an escape from your professional life but as a powerful tool that enhances your experiences and expands your opportunities.

In 1282, eyeglasses were the cutting-edge technology of the day, introduced in Northern Italy when Dante Alighieri[2] was in his early twenties. As a progressive thinker unafraid of new ideas, Dante likely saw the value in this innovation. Imagine someone offering young Dante a tool that could help him see more clearly—it's hard to picture him rejecting it for a more "natural" approach, especially given his bold critiques of the corrupt priests in his Divine Comedy. Dante was a visionary, not limited by the norms of his time, and would have recognized how new tools could enhance human potential. So, would you turn down the new technology eyeglasses if they were suggested?

Throughout this book, you'll discover how VR can revolutionize your approach to work, unlocking unprecedented levels of productivity, creativity, fulfillment, and collaboration. Integrating VR into your daily routine allows you to transcend conventional limitations, opening doors to innovative ways of thinking, working, and living.

We'll redefine what it means to *work* and *go to work* by critically examining and discarding outdated rituals, habits, and narratives. This isn't just about seeing the bigger picture; it's about realizing that your current work routine might only feel secure because it offers the illusion of status and stability. It's time to break free from that illusion and embrace a new, more fulfilling way of working.

Now, you can make conscious choices about how and where you want to live and work, using all the tools available to create a more productive and fulfilling professional life.

In these pages, you'll learn how to design a process and daily structure that allows you to purposefully enter a state of deep work, even achieving flow. This structure will help you manage the immediate pressures and demands of your professional and personal life more effectively. It will give you more time for what matters most and teach you to navigate your days with intention, steering your life toward goals and dreams that resonate deeply with you.

The Environment

Alex had always been captivated by the mountains. He spent hours watching climbing videos and gazing at pictures of the "crux" of a super tough climb, dreaming of the day he would be the one in the video. The challenge and beauty of these fantastic monuments called to him, offering freedom from the teasing and embarrassment he faced at school.

As he grew older, Alex's passion for climbing became a way of life. He became an avid climber, dedicating every spare moment to exploring new trails and scaling more difficult cliffs. The risks were significant, but the joy and connection to nature were unmatched. Climbing wasn't just a hobby; it was his refuge, where he could escape the pressures of the modern world.

For years, Alex lived out of his van, chasing the next flow state offered by an awesome climb and reveling in the simplicity of his nomadic lifestyle. But as he approached his thirties, his situation began to weigh on him. He loved the freedom of the mountains, but he couldn't live in his van and climb forever. The world was moving forward, and he felt he was standing still.

With all its promises, technology often felt like a foreign language to Alex. While it offered incredible tools and resources, it also brought about a relentless pace that terrified him. The tools designed to make life easier complicate it further, adding layers of stress and pressure. He felt a growing disconnect, as if the world was moving too fast for him to catch up.

One evening, after a grueling day on the mountain, Alex found himself sitting by the campfire, the flickering flames mirroring the turmoil within him. He loved the mountains, but a nagging fear kept burning in him—the fear of being left behind. As technology raced ahead, he felt increasingly out of place, ill-equipped to keep up. The thought of trading his climbing gear for a desk job horrified him, but the fear of being excluded, like in school, and the inability to support himself weighed heavily on his mind. As the fire crackled and loudly "popped," Alex suddenly realized he had felt this way before. It was fear, plain and simple.

He had faced bullies before, back in school, where the taunts and intimidation were relentless. He learned early on that the only way to deal with them was to stand up and fight back. Now, as he sat by the campfire after a grueling day on the mountain, he realized that fear was the toughest bully of them all. His years in the mountains had taught him that fear was a fierce competitor, one that demanded confrontation and resolution—just like those bullies from his past. Alex knew that, just as he had to face down those schoolyard bullies, he had to stand up to this fear head-on. His climbing buddy Stu, someone he admired for his sharp intellect and wide-ranging knowledge, often reminded him of Ralph Waldo Emerson's words:

"Do the thing you fear, and the death of fear is certain."

This wasn't just about technology; it was about the unknown. The mountains had always been his sanctuary, where he faced fear head-on with every climb. Now, the digital world loomed before him like an impossible peak, with its ever-changing landscape and intimidating terminology. But Alex understood that, just as he had tackled countless climbs before, he had to approach this new challenge with the same resolve.

He realized that mastering fear wasn't a one-time victory but a constant balancing act, like traversing a narrow ledge with a sheer drop on either side. It required vigilance, every moment, to survive and grow. This new challenge wasn't just a barrier; it was "a new project to send," as climbers say—a challenge to be faced and conquered.

The next day, Alex descended the mountain with a newfound determination. He connected with his buddy Stu, who he knew was also some "tech whiz," and asked for guidance. Over the following months, Alex discovered the power of VR for accelerated learning and engagement. Immersing himself in new technologies, he found tools that enhanced, rather than overshadowed, his life. Alex seamlessly integrated these advancements with his passion for climbing, using technology to map routes and connect with fellow climbers. This journey not only broadened his horizons but also deepened his love for both climbing and technology.

But the truth was his new journey was challenging. Sometimes, he felt overwhelmed and frustrated with all the Bullshit, longing for the simplicity of his van and the mountains. Slowly, he began to see the broad possibilities of combining his passion with the digital world. He envisioned a future where he could have the best of both worlds—climbing and staying connected, pursuing his passion while building a sustainable family life.

One evening, months later, Alex found himself again at the summit of his favorite peak. The route had this gnarly crux that he'd been working on for weeks, and in his words, "I nailed the beta and cruised through it. The rock was in perfect condition, and I felt super solid on all the holds." As the sun set, casting a golden glow over the landscape, he gazed out at the vast expanse before him; the view was breathtaking, and time seemed to slow as he was overcome with a profound sense of peace, acceptance, and appreciation, a reminder of the importance of climbing and the mountains in his life - this was his classroom. Here, he wasn't just a climber, a husband, or a tech novice; he was becoming a whole person who had faced his fears and found a way to move forward.

In that moment of Flow, Alex realized that progress wasn't just about keeping up with his new neighbors, the exploding climbing industry, or technology; it was about letting go of the things in his life he had been taught or conditioned to think were important and necessary. It was about letting go of the old and embracing advancements without losing himself in the process. The mountains had taught him resilience, patience, and the value of taking things one step at a time. These were lessons he could apply to every aspect of his life.

Returning from his climb, Alex felt a renewed sense of purpose. He continued to explore how VR technology could enhance his work and life, discovering tools that allowed for deeper focus and platforms that connected him with a community of like-minded individuals. He had found a way to navigate the terrain ahead, blending the wisdom of the mountains with the potential of technology. The fear of being left behind had transformed into a journey of self-discovery and growth, proving that even the most daunting peaks could be conquered one step at a time.

Let Go and Lighten Up

Before we can move forward, you...my dear reader, need to lighten up —let go of the Bullshit... it's heavy, and it stinks. To do this, you must first authentically distinguish it. The "It" is how you relate to "work" and "going to work," which is based on habits, rituals, and old stories that you have blithely adopted, accepted, and followed. By recognizing and releasing these outdated patterns, you can embrace a new way of working and living. Now, I realize that while it may be simple as a concept, it is far from easy. These beliefs and patterns are well-worn and, to some degree, work for you and provide comfort. But come on, man...

If you read the wisdom of the Stoics, you may know what Epictetus famously said:

> *"If there is something in life you think you should be, then you should be that."*[3]

This quote underscores the importance of pursuing your true calling and aligning your actions with your deepest values and aspirations.

Metaphors - Power Tools

As I explored in my first book, metaphors are potent tools for understanding complex ideas. Coming from an engineering background rather than a literary one, I find metaphors to be efficient and effective communication tools— more impactful than perfectly crafted prose. They simplify complex concepts while adding depth and imagery. Just as a power tool cuts through materials precisely, metaphors cut through complexity, making intricate ideas more accessible to grasp and convey.

Experts like George Lakoff and Steven Pinker argue that our thinking is inherently metaphorical, shaping our understanding and communication. A well-crafted metaphor can unlock a wealth of knowledge, providing clarity on complex and subtle ideas.

Take, for example, the metaphor of parental guidance as a *map*. A good map doesn't just give directions; it shows multiple paths, highlights the topography of a journey's highs and lows, and reflects environmental changes, like seasonal freezes or tides. This metaphor suggests that parents don't need to provide exact instructions but offer a nuanced understanding of the journey ahead.

In this chapter, I will expand on the metaphor of a *map* you create to guide your working life. This map will help you navigate individual concepts and offer a comprehensive framework that weaves together VR, cognitive, cultural, psychological, and narrative dimensions.

Metaphor - Society's Demands

Imagine your life as a sprawling, mountainous terrain. Most of your journey is spent scaling steep, unforgiving peaks and navigating treacherous walls. Challenging and arduous landscapes symbolize your relentless pursuit of productivity and economic success, driven by societal pressures to climb higher and higher. Every step you take focuses on overcoming obstacles and pushing yourself to reach the summit, maximizing your position and status as society demands.

However, sparsely throughout this rugged terrain are small, hidden valleys and serene, picturesque meadows. These rare, tranquil spots represent the moments you take to genuinely enjoy life. These meadows are lush green, vibrant, and bathed in sunlight, offering brief but precious respite from your strenuous climb. Yet, they are few and far between, and accessing them requires deliberate effort to step off the adrenaline express.

In this metaphoric landscape, the demanding ascent consumes most of your energy and effort, leaving only fleeting opportunities to pause, relax, and savor the simple joys of life. Finding and appreciating these serene meadows amidst the vast, challenging mountains is essential to having the energy to pursue the things most important.

Max Tegmark, a leading physicist and cosmologist, is known for his innovative work in AI, consciousness, and the nature of reality. As a tenured professor at MIT and co-founder of the Future of Life Institute, Tegmark offers a compelling analogy in his book, *Life 3.0: Being Human in the Age of Artificial Intelligence.*[4] He asks us to imagine human skills and knowledge as a vast landscape. Essential and basic tools like math and science occupy the lowlands, while more advanced concepts like calculus, algebra, and quantum mechanics rise to form foothills and peaks.

Tegmark uses the idea of rising waters to represent the rapid advancement of technology and knowledge. As the waters rise, they first cover the most basic tools and skills, making them obsolete—just as personal computers replaced handheld calculators and typewriters. This metaphor highlights how technology continuously evolves, overtaking older methods.

The rising waters symbolize the democratization of technology, leveling the playing field as new tools become more accessible. This shift mirrors the transformative impact of the printing press and digital photography, revolutionizing access to information and art. However, this democratization has collided with outdated urban planning and transportation systems, intensifying the struggle to secure livable spaces.

For the past 50 years, economic pressures have driven people to relocate to large, aging cities, creating densely packed urban areas marked by traffic congestion and towering high-rises. This relentless competition for space has led to daily frustrations, what I call "the Bullshit," characterized by inefficiencies like traffic jams and endless queues.

As we stand at a crucial juncture in the digital era, innovation pushes us to adapt and seek higher ground, both literally and figuratively. We're forced to reassess our strategies and navigate modern challenges with outdated infrastructures post-Second World War II. This section explores how contemporary technologies and the networks they create are reshaping our lives, challenging us to move beyond the limitations of our physical world and the inefficiencies.

A New Map

By leveraging the capabilities of advanced technologies, we can reclaim time once consumed by the Bullshit - the so-called "real" necessities of life. Technologies such as online meetings, shopping, exercise, entertainment, and social connections are dramatically improved with the added transformative nature of VR and AR. It's not merely the change in the venue from screen to VR; it's the rendering capabilities harnessing Moores's Law, which now allows for the manipulation and sharing of data inside an immersive experience that shreds the old "Dropbox days."

This newfound time affords us the opportunity to engage in activities that nourish the mind and body, allowing for a richer, more fulfilling life and giving access to what some call the true meaning of life. If you take on this challenge and VR technology, you, too, may follow this new MAP, which is merely an acronym for Mastery, Autonomy, and Personal connections/purpose.

In fact, Herman Narula, author of Virtual Society and co-founder and CEO of Improbable, discusses the significant mental and physiological benefits of using VR. He explains that VR can act like a "mental gym,"[5] providing a space for users to exercise their minds and enhance cognitive function. By engaging in immersive experiences, individuals can develop skills, improve mental resilience, and achieve a sense of accomplishment and connection, like physical exercise strengthens the body. He suggests that the true goal of the metaverse isn't just immersion but achieving a sense of presence—where users feel their actions have real significance in the virtual world. This engagement can enhance mental well-being and cognitive function by providing a space for meaningful interaction and creativity that meet our underlying psychological needs outlined in SDT (Self Determination Theory)."[6]

As we navigate this technological tide, you can rely on this MAP to guide you towards deep work and flow—states essential for achieving mastery and exceptional performance in your field, rather than merely getting by with busy work and multitasking.

The strategic use of VR technology also affords us the autonomy to design our days around work that matters, meaningful connections, physical wellness, and intellectual growth.

MAP is both a metaphor and an acronym. As an acronym, it refers to the key elements of Self-Determination Theory (mastery, autonomy, and personal connections). While not perfect, this theory is a powerful way to understand how to self-motivate and accomplish great things.

We stand at the cusp of a significant shift in human existence, moving from a state of perpetual labor[7] to one that prioritizes our values and aspirations and appreciates this amazing thing called the flow state, an ecstatic state that was, until recently, granted to very few humans.

This technological evolution fosters a society that is more inclusive and equitable, challenging the notion that embracing digital worlds detaches us from reality. On the contrary, as the telephone enhanced our ability to connect, AR and VR technologies promise to deepen our connections and broaden our worldviews. Our future calls with a promise of focused intentionality, free from the excessive noise of our previous constraints.

Now, you may be saying, look, this is the same story, just new technology; why and how is this "new tech" different? "

Well, the emergence of VR technologies signifies both a transition to new digital heights and an invitation to explore entirely new dimensions of existence.

With the advent of VR technologies, the concept of 'going to work' can be accurately described as being transformed, transcending physical boundaries to the extent that there is no longer a 'going' in 'going to work.'

An authentic transformation, such as seen in the physical transformation of a liquid to a gas, after which there is no liquid...Not the hyped-up, so-called "feel-good" transformations used by weekend seminars.

This revolutionary shift brings the mountain to us in ways Francis Bacon could never have imagined, eliminating the traditional commute and reshaping our daily lives.

4

VR, THE SAFE SPACE

As the last member of the team reached the summit, the crisp mountain air was filled with cheers, hugs, and high-fives. But for Alex, something deeper stirred. Surrounded by his team amid this breathtaking landscape, he felt a profound sense of connection. Pausing to take it all in, he drew in a deep, full breath that seemed to open up a part of him he hadn't accessed before. In that moment, he wasn't just appreciating the view or the accomplishment—he was tapping into a primal, visceral connection to life itself. It wasn't just about his life that day but the essence of life—a powerful sense of oneness.

As Alex drove back from the climb, with each mile, however, the excitement, the fist bumps, and the hugs faded, and he was left with a void inside. During the long, slow route down, the conversation with his "clients," a word he put up with, included curious concepts with which he had little knowledge and were just out of his reach. Physcology, political science, and philosophy were unfamiliar and unexplored, and he often argued with himself that he would never need them. At this point, he had to turn the car radio off so it didn't encroach on the increasingly loud conversation he was having in his head. But he brushed it off because he thought he was often just one of "those kids" who hated school and loved climbing; it was as simple as that, or was it? As he grew older, the questions from the empty void grew louder, "Is this all there is?"

Alex Lowe's words, "There are two kinds of climbers: those who climb because their heart sings when they're in the mountains, and all the rest,"[1] reveal so much, but what he doesn't show is that those whose hearts sing in the mountains, much of their early lives in the 19th and 20th century was a demoralizing experience - but for climbing.

For so many people, the traditional classrooms and 19th-century hier-archical "so-called" educational programs actually harmed their self-worth. When you're 8-18, this self-image becomes baked in. Choosing between the humiliation of not keeping up with classmates in an environment that doesn't work for you and one that draws the very best from you is an easy decision.

There is just too much evidence now that proves we all learn differently[2]. In many cases, particularly with the more subtle learning disabilities, children who are at the most vulnerable come to believe they are somehow "less than" someone who gets better grades or has the most friends.

Thanks to AR and VR today, education can be democratized. One can be immersed in an environment, free from the competitive distractions of others, free to focus on the work itself. And aided by AI, they can work in a program designed just for them.

The impact of VR in education is profound and promises to remove the stigma of a learning disability or social phobia issue. VR and AR will keep children fully occupied for the appropriate time, allowing them time to learn to socialize with other kids - in person, at super-vised meet-ups, with kids just like them.

VR for the Elderly

It's not just the younger generation struggling to fit into "traditional systems." As hundreds of thousands of older men and women move into the later stages of their lives, they find that the conventional "old folks home" doesn't work for them.

This truth hit me hard in the shadow of my father's recent Alzheimer's diagnosis. The weight of my new responsibilities pressed down on me. My father and I had forged a deep friendship after my mother's passing—a bond that had become a constant source of comfort and support in my life. He wasn't just my father but my best man at my wedding.

As his condition worsened, I found myself stepping into a new role as his caregiver and devoted son, a role that demanded everything I could give. This realization became painfully clear one crisp October day when I returned to my hometown of Markham. The sharp autumn air, mixed with the warm sunlight illuminating the brilliantly colored leaves, sparked a glimmer of hope in me, even as I grappled with the reality of our situation.

Now, seeing him in the assisted living community just a short distance from our family home was both shocking and heart-wrenching. It had been a year since he moved in, and the man who once proudly walked those well-maintained grounds now struggled to manage even with a walker.

Dad is a "hugger," but this hug, meant to be a comforting gesture, was overshadowed by the stark reality of his condition and gnawing guilt that I had encouraged him to move to this place. In hindsight, it sometimes felt more for my convenience than his well-being. His early remarks about the community, "It's full of old people with walkers," haunted me as I watched his rapid decline.

Our time together was priceless, often spent on the way to hockey games or practice. During these moments, my curiosity would lead me to ask why he chose his career path. His answer was always simple—he wanted to contribute to society's well-being by cleaning the air we breathe. I still smile when I recall one particular explanation he gave me as a child.

He was also an engineer and a business partner selling industrial air filtration equipment. He mentioned selling dust collectors and scrubbers; to my young mind, this meant he held a janitorial post for big businesses. I pictured a scrubber as a guy with a giant brush and a dust collector as someone who ... spent his day collecting dust.

The assisted living community where my father now resides is just a stone's throw away from our family home. We chose it because of its proximity to his friends and favorite coffee spots, hoping to preserve some sense of normalcy for him. But as I stood there, looking at the man who once filled my life with strength and guidance, I realized how much had changed. The traditional solutions—whether for the young or the old—no longer fit the reality of our times. As I faced this painful transition with my father, I began to see the broader implications of how we, as a society, need to rethink the systems and structures we've long taken for granted.

This is where VR offers a glimpse into the future—a tool not just for the young but also for those like my father, who deserve more than what the traditional paths can offer. VR has the potential to create spaces where memories are preserved, connections are deepened, and the limitations of age are challenged, offering new ways to experience life even in its later stages. My father and our journey together have shown me the urgent need for innovation in caring for and connecting with those who have given us so much.

As I left the community that evening, the cold wind felt like an accusation, urging me to confront the memories and decisions that had led us here. Driven by an unexplained longing, I detoured past our old family home, only to find it diminished; its vibrancy faded like an old photograph. Continuing on to my old high school, memories I had buried deep resurfaced, particularly those of my final year there.

Cool is No Longer Cool

High school was a time when being among the "cool kids" and part of the popular hockey crowd brought its own set of challenges. For a while, I was caught up in that world, but the influence of my parents eventually led me to prioritize education over being part of the gang. This decision pissed off my former "so-called" friends, isolating me from the gang I once thought was everything.

But the consequences of that choice came down hard on me in a violent confrontation with the gang's leaders—a memory that still sends shivers down my spine. Being physically assaulted, masked as male bonding, left a deep scar, a painful reminder of the cost of trying to be cool with the wrong people.

It was a typical cold and gray Saturday afternoon in Ontario, and I remember my spirits lifting when I got a call from one of the gang leaders inviting me to a party to watch the game. I thought that maybe, just maybe, my shift away from the hockey crowd was being recognized positively.

When I entered the house, I was greeted by only the two gang leaders. There was no party, just the two laughing and joking as they commanded me to "get a beer." The next moments are hazy, perhaps mercifully so, but the sense of betrayal and the cold sweat of fear still lingers. They preyed on my weakness—the desperate need to be liked and accepted—and before I knew it, they performed increasingly violent WWE wrestling moves on me, laughing and cheering each other on with every blow.

At first, I tried to downplay the brutality, convincing myself that this was some strange rite of passage within the gang. But the stench of beer, blood, and hatred quickly shattered my delusions. These guys were in bad shape; their attacks were broken up by bouts of recovery and more beer. Pinned to the floor, panic-stricken and on the verge of tears, I tried to escape. But the final blow came in the form of a reverse headlock—the biggest gang member using his drunken strength to slam my head onto the hardwood floor. And then, darkness.

When I regained consciousness, perhaps minutes later, I found myself alone. My nose was bleeding, one shoe was missing, and a booming headache pierced through the disoriented haze. Barely able to stand, I stumbled out the door and limped the mile home in the frigid 40-degree temperatures.

That incident looms over my past like a dark cloud, shaping my perspectives and leaving a profound impact that lingers today. As I drive through the familiar streets of our old neighborhood, the painful memory echoes through time. I can still see myself limping towards our front door, shivering from the cold and the traumatic assault.

The weeks and months that followed were a blur of confusion, humiliation, and isolation. I found solace in my studies but not much else. The pain of that day, both physical and emotional, has never entirely left me. It's a reminder of how deeply the need for acceptance can lead us down dangerous paths and how, in the end, "cool" is never really cool.

These experiences, both recent and from my youth, have taught me the profound impact our environment and associations have on our well-being. Observing my father's decline and reflecting on my own past, I've come to understand the subtle yet powerful influence of our surroundings. This insight, further deepened by the work of psychologist Tim Wilson and his exploration of the unconscious mind, has been a guiding light in navigating these challenging times.

Wilson's research[3] underscores our environment's significant role in shaping our mood, behavior, and overall mental state, often without our conscious realization. This understanding has helped me come to terms with my past and opened my eyes to the potential of augmented and virtual Reality in creating spaces that enhance our quality of life.

Discovering Tim Wilson's insights into the unconscious mind further supported the map I was developing.

His research—particularly the idea that much of our behavior and emotional responses operate beneath our conscious awareness—helped explain life patterns that had long puzzled me. I began to see how my inclination to withdraw and isolate when I was part of a group, or "gang," wasn't a conscious choice but a deeply ingrained response, a survival mechanism hardwired. This realization brought a newfound compassion and understanding to my struggles with social settings, allowing me to approach my inner battles more empathetically.

But here's where I hit a wall: the prevailing advice to "be aware of your thoughts" frustrates me. As engineers who like fixing stuff, with all the advancements in science—FMRIs, AI, VR/AR, neuro-implants, and so on—are we still expected to believe that awareness is the best we can do? For me, awareness often arrives too late, a dim light in the darkness after I've isolated myself. Once I'm in the clutches of that cold, lonely space, mere awareness isn't enough to pull me out.

This is why I've embraced VR as the living embodiment of Professor Wilson's research. VR isn't just a tool; it's a transformative force that allows me to craft environments designed to counteract those unconscious patterns that have held me captive. In the immersive world of VR, the environment becomes the architect of change, guiding my mind away from destructive, automatic responses and leading me toward healing and growth.

This approach has been nothing short of revolutionary in navigating the emotional pitfalls of my father's illness. It has also helped to reshape my interactions and made me a more empathetic friend, son, and colleague. By intentionally designing the virtual spaces I inhabit, I've unearthed tools that have freed me from the unconscious scripts that once dictated my reactions to stress and change.

AR and VR extend far beyond mere escapism; they can revolutionize how we educate, care for older people, and approach our daily lives. For me, VR has been more than just a refuge from the stresses of caregiving and work—it has become a sanctuary of relaxation and a proactive tool for mental well-being.

Augmented Reality, too, has proven its worth, particularly in the workplace. Virtual meetings that feel as personal and engaging as face-to-face interactions mean that remote work no longer means a sacrifice in connection. These experiences have convinced me that AR and VR are not just technological marvels but the keys to designing physical and digital environments that enrich our lives and support our overall well-being.

In a world where simple awareness often falls short, AR and VR provide the means to seize control of our environments and, in doing so, our lives. They empower us to transcend the limitations of our unconscious minds and build real and virtual worlds where we can truly thrive.

As we move forward, it's time to explore how these technologies lay the foundation for a whole new way to work—one that breaks free from outdated structures and opens the door to unprecedented possibilities. The next chapter will delve into this exciting transformation, where the boundaries of what work can be are redefined, and the future is shaped not just by the tools we use but by the environments we create.

5

THE IMPACT OF OUR ENVIRONMENT

Intolerance for Bullshit

After 30 years, I'm now convinced that this poly-tribe of engineering professionals, of which I am immensely proud to be part share a distinctive trait. It may well be an evolutionary genetic mutation, with rapid pattern recognition and deductive reasoning- we possess a severe intolerance for the dumbed down, institutionally morass, the poorly designed and short-sighted processes, which force us to "go so slowly," that it triggers profound irritation upon exposure.

The collective noun for this should be "Bullshit" is a massive and messy category, but while I'm referring to it as institutional inefficiencies, it also includes the subsets of legacy practices that always and unwittingly force you to go slow and waste time.

The Liberation VR and AR Offer

My enthusiasm for leading initiatives in VR and AR stems from the liberation these technologies offer from the encumbrances that particular kind of bullshit brings with it. In the realm of VR and AR, the value placed on an individual's creativity, insights, and innovation eclipses conventional markers of status such as job titles, office locations, academic backgrounds, nationality, ethnicity, physical appearance, or other superficial measures.

I argue that by eliminating these distractions—akin to clearing away the proverbial 'bullshit' that includes daily commutes of three hours, for instance—we gain the freedom and energy to fully express ourselves, to emerge from our shells, and to thrive as the individuals we aspire to be. Persisting in a conventional setting rife with these impediments is as futile as attempting to swim through a lake clogged with seaweed, driftwood, and, quite literally, waste.

VR and AR as 'Scrubbers'

Consider AR/VR technology as a metaphorical 'scrubber'—not a person wielding a brush, but a device designed to purify. Industrial scrubbers cleanse hazardous gases from factory emissions, such as the sulfur dioxide (SO_2) and nitrogen oxides (NOx) produced by coal combustion, by using either liquid solutions or dry sorbents to capture and neutralize pollutants. Much like these scrubbers clear the air of toxins, VR and AR technologies can cleanse our working environments of the metaphorical pollutants that hinder our efficiency and well-being.

This transformative potential of AR and VR is rooted in the convergence of four technological advancements in the early 2000s. Together, they have set the stage for us to employ these technologies in truly revolutionary ways, heralding a new era of efficiency and innovation free from the constraints of traditional workplace 'bullshit.'

The Four Pillars of Technological Advancement

The underpinnings of my argument are firstly drawn from the extensive research highlighting the profound impact of our adaptive unconscious on our thought processes and actions. This is complemented by the second pillar: the well-established body of research on biophilia, which demonstrates how exposure to natural environments can significantly enhance our mental well-being.

The third point emphasizes the practical benefits of AR and VR. These technologies offer a practical escape from the daily grind of institutional inefficiencies, such as battling rush-hour traffic or waking up in the early morning hours to catch a flight for a brief meeting. By integrating AR and VR into our routines, we can bypass these time-consuming obstacles, preserving our zeal for life that might otherwise be dimmed by mundane rituals and outdated practices.

The fourth dimension of this discussion focuses on the evolution of the technology itself. Until the turn of the millennium, virtual reality remained more of a tantalizing concept than a tangible reality, surrounded by hype yet underdelivered. However, propelled by the relentless pace of technological advancement—exemplified by Moore's Law—the quality of VR and AR has soared while their costs and physical burdens have diminished.

Misconceptions about Continuous Usage

As a side note: Whenever I mention AR/VR/MR, please keep in mind that I'm referring to their usage for intentional, focused, and strategic durations. There's a common misconception that this cutting-edge technology might be so enthralling and captivating that we could fall into the habit of using it incessantly. But let's clear up this misapprehension. Given that AR and VR are proactive and engaging platforms, in contrast with TV or video, which are more laid back and passive, continuous use would be physically draining. If relaxation is what you're after, you'd find chilling on a sofa with the TV remote a far better choice.

VR offers us the opportunity to experience the extraordinary, to design lives of our choosing, and to immerse ourselves in the vast potential of our existence—recapturing the boundless imagination and joy we experienced as children.

While AR and VR technologies have the power to transform our lives and redefine our workspaces, it is imperative to approach them with a mindset of balance and mindful usage. Prolonged exposure can lead to fatigue, both mentally and physically, potentially hindering the productivity and creativity we seek to enhance. Therefore, establishing clear boundaries and setting intentional limits on usage time is essential. By creating a structured routine that incorporates breaks and opportunities for real-world interactions, users can prevent burnout and maintain a healthy equilibrium. Practicing this discipline not only preserves the novelty and effectiveness of these tools but also encourages a holistic lifestyle where digital and physical worlds coexist harmoniously, fostering both innovation and well-being.

My Journey to Engineering

This pursuit of engaging, autonomous work environments, free from the constraints of cubicles and office politics, is what initially drew me to engineering. This desire led me to work in Saudi Arabia shortly after graduation, seeking experiences beyond the conventional office setting. Before I fully understood the concepts of motivation and self-determination theory, I often felt out of place because of my aversion to traditional office life, including its politics and monotonous routines.

Discovering Freedom in Saudi Arabia

In Saudi Arabia, I cherished the early mornings, setting out in a Chevrolet Caprice before the sun's intense rays and the desert heat set in. Those moments, akin to the mythical beauty of Artemis at dawn, represented the essence of freedom and exploration that I yearned for in my work and life.

After sunrise, I would drive over two hours along the coast of the Arabian Gulf towards Al Jubail or Al Khafji. These cities were expanding rapidly under the guidance of the Royal Commission, essentially managed by the major American engineering firm, Bechtel. The route, a two-lane highway, often meandered through sand drifts, with occasional camel crossings and mysteriously abandoned Mercedes, each with its own untold story of a crash or empty fuel tank.

The drive itself was mesmerizing, bordered by the sparkling turquoise waters of the Gulf on one side and the endless expanse of the desert on the other. This environment was not just a backdrop for my commute; it was a source of restoration and fascination, offering a profound sense of presence and rejuvenation.

The Crowd Stopper Experiment: An Engineer's Quest for Beach Time

Saudi Arabia in the 1980s, particularly the Eastern Province and the ARAMCO complex in Dhahran, attracted a peculiar breed of engineers—rebels in button-down shirts who had little patience for corporate bureaucracy and an insatiable curiosity for all things mechanical. I was one of them.

I had a couple of close friends who, like me, had traded the rigid structures of corporate America for the freedom to experiment, explore, and occasionally cause trouble. We built distillation rigs to make 100% proof alcohol using "surplus" equipment from the well-stocked ARAMCO labs and refineries. We designed bizarre contraptions with questionable effectiveness but undeniable ingenuity. And then there was the infamous "Crowd Stopper", a device that, in hindsight, should be written off as youthful misadventure.

But at the time? It was science. It was innovation. And, most importantly, it was our ticket to the beach.

Life at ARAMCO and the Half Moon Bay Problem

The ARAMCO compound was a few miles from my modest apartment in Dammam. At the time, it housed about 9,500 residents and had the feel of a West Coast summer camp—low-rise bungalows, palm-lined roads, and a close-knit community of expats. Life revolved around work, and with *only one day off per week*—Saturday—free time was precious.

The best way to spend it? Windsurfing or scuba diving at Half Moon Bay, just past the ubiquitous Bin Laden grocery stores, near the Meridian Hotel.

The problem? Embassy parties.

Not the glamorous, spy-filled Middle Eastern galas you see in James Bond movies. No, these were crowded, alcohol-hunting social gatherings at the tired old ARAMCO administration building. Worse still, when these parties were held, the compound gates were closed, trapping us inside and keeping us from the beach.

It was an injustice of the highest order, and we were out to change that—with science.

Enter Dave: The Mad Scientist of Dhahran

The mastermind behind this particular scheme was Dave, a mechanical engineer from MIT, whom I had worked with a couple of times as a client.

Dave was a character straight out of a Sir Arthur Conan Doyle novel —a disheveled, slightly overweight, 6′5″ figure with long, shaggy hair and a greying beard, resembling a scruffy Sherlock Holmes. He dabbled in mind-altering substances, fancied himself an inventor, and was a surprisingly good musician. His most prized possession? A top-of-the-line Moog synthesizer, which he claimed was a "surplus" piece from ARAMCO.

One evening, during a sidiki (homemade alcohol) testing session, he revealed his grand plan.

His idea, inspired by a friend at MIT involved in military research, was based on the use of low-frequency inaudible sound waves for crowd control. The military hypothesis was that these waves could disrupt gatherings by creating discomfort—a non-lethal, stealthy way to disperse people.

But Dave had a much more sinister application in mind.

According to him, at a very specific frequency and volume, it was theoretically possible to create a standing wave in the human anal sphincter and ascending colon. This frequency would simultaneously force open these passageways while disrupting the natural "pucker" reflex, leading to one inevitable outcome: mass, uncontrollable defecation.

A weaponized brown note.

Theoretically, if it worked, the embassy party would end in a mess so catastrophic that the attendees would flee, leaving the compound gates unguarded—allowing us to escape to the beach.

A noble application of brilliant engineering.

The Setup: Testing the Brown Note

I arrived at Dave's California-style one-bedroom bungalow around 7 AM, just before the heat kicked in. He was already buzzing with excitement, loading his white Mitsubishi pickup truck with equipment.

The key component? A military-grade loudspeaker that looked like an old-fashioned foghorn, gifted to him by another MIT friend—a mechanical engineering grad student named Boses (a name that would later become eerily familiar in the world of acoustics).

As I passed through the ARAMCO gates, the guard informed me, "The compound will be closed for several hours today."

We'll see about that, I thought.

The weather was perfect—85°F, low humidity, light breeze. An ideal day for windsurfing, assuming we could successfully execute Project Crowd Stopper.

We parked across from the recreation center, out of sight of the party, and began setting up. Dave, with the concentration of a mad scientist, adjusted dials, checked cables, and muttered calculations under his breath.

Finally, after an hour of meticulous preparation, he looked up and grinned mischievously.

"The game is afoot!" he declared.

The Execution: An Unexpected Plot Twist

As the embassy party continued inside, we crouched behind the pickup, watching and waiting.

Then, with an almost ceremonial flick of the switch, Dave activated the device.

Silence.

No visible reaction.

We exchanged glances. Dave adjusted the frequency, tweaked the volume, and tried again. Still nothing.

I strolled over to the gathering, expecting chaos—or at least some visible discomfort. But to my dismay, the party continued completely unaffected.

Back at the truck, Dave was frantically reconfiguring wires, adjusting dials, and swearing under his breath. Another attempt.

Still nothing.

For twenty agonizing minutes, we watched, hoping for at least one distressed diplomat to clutch his stomach and run for the door. But our grand scheme had failed spectacularly.

Dave, visibly frustrated, sighed and shook his head. Then, in a moment of sheer brilliance, he turned to me and muttered:

"I knew they were a bunch of tight-asses."

Without missing a beat, I delivered the only logical response:

"No shit, Sherlock."

And just like that, we packed up our failed experiment and headed for the beach—with nothing to show for our efforts except a fantastic story and a newfound appreciation for the gastrointestinal resilience of American diplomats.

Liberation from Conventional Work Settings

My decision to live and work in this unique setting puzzled my colleagues and superiors from Wisconsin, the headquarters of The Trane Company, my then-employer. Their bewilderment, often expressed out of my earshot, questioned the appeal of such a location. Yet, for me, it was this exact immersion in an environment so distinctly removed from the competitive, efficiency-driven cultures of North America that I found liberating. It offered the autonomy and simplicity I longed for, akin to Thoreau's retreat to Walden Pond or Muir's explorations of Yosemite[1], providing a canvas where my best self could emerge, unencumbered.

This personal odyssey underscored the undeniable impact our environment has on our mental state and effectiveness. Just as historical figures found clarity and inspiration in nature, my experiences in the Saudi desert highlighted the power of surroundings to enhance our well-being and productivity.

The Ethical Considerations of AR and VR

However, as we navigate the potential of Augmented Reality (AR) and Virtual Reality (VR), it's prudent to also consider the challenges these technologies may pose. Reflecting on the futuristic scenarios depicted in Steven Spielberg's *The Minority Report*[2], some may question the darker aspects of AR and VR environments. Indeed, the issue isn't just the prospect of pervasive and intrusive advertising as portrayed in the film, but the precision with which such advertising could target and exploit our vulnerabilities.

The ethical implications of technology's role in our lives are increasingly evident. Tragic narratives, often dominated by acts of violence, only occasionally shed light on underlying factors such as gambling addiction—a stark reminder of technology's potential to sway human behavior dramatically. A case in point is a devastating incident involving a 42-year-old entrepreneur who, driven to despair by gambling, tragically ended the lives of his family and himself, leaving behind a note that pointed to his addiction as the cause. Such stories underscore the urgent need for a balanced and ethical approach to the integration of advanced technologies into our daily lives, highlighting the fine line between innovation and exploitation.

The Destructive Nature of Gambling Addiction

Among the ruins of a life undone by gambling, police discovered evidence of $225,000 in torn-up casino markers—a grim testament to the ravaging effects of addiction within the alluring yet merciless setting of Las Vegas. It's a stark realization that gambling doesn't just erode the individual's life; it has the potential to devastate the lives of those around them, echoing the sentiment that gambling is uniquely catastrophic, capable of destroying not just the gambler but also the lives of loved ones.

The financial wreckage left in the wake of this addiction was substantial. The individual's business was reportedly drowning under a $500,000 debt incurred through gambling, while three credit cards found at the scene bore an additional $60,000 debt. Despite some attributing the tragedy to personal failings rather than the manipulative designs of gambling machines and casino environments, emerging research tells a different story.

Natasha Dow Schüll, an MIT professor specializing in gambling addiction, sheds light on how electronic gambling machines and their algorithms are engineered to ensnare players into prolonged sessions. Her research reveals that even a glance at the screens found in many establishments can profoundly influence thoughts and behavior, underscoring the sinister ways in which technology and the environment conspire to manipulate user behavior.

Schüll's findings, supported by numerous case studies[3], illustrate a chilling reality: under certain conditions, anyone could find themselves ensnared by similar compulsions. This notion is bolstered by academic consensus (free from commercial interests) affirming the significant impact of both digital and physical environments on our psychological state and actions.

The Influence of Tech Giants on Human Behavior

Contrastingly, the gambling industry, flush with resources, often presents a sanitized narrative of gambling's impact. The alarming truth, however, is that leading tech companies—Google, Facebook, Apple, and Microsoft—are actively recruiting top academic talents, redirecting pioneering research towards developing AI that can exploit human behavior for profit. Jaron Lanier, a critical voice in tech ethics now at Microsoft, warns of the internet's capacity to induce a trance-like state, dulling critical thinking and promoting automatic, feedback-loop-driven behavior. He says:

> "When you watch the same kind of thing over and over again, your brain falls into this mesmerized state, which I compare to a trancelike state, that's being encouraged by the internet. It's not that the internet is turning us into idiots, but it is making us act like idiots because we're not thinking. We're automatically driven by this feedback that's happening from these loops that get established."[4]

Our Environments Shape Us

As this exploration concludes its first segment, the overarching argument crystallizes: our environments, both digital and physical, exert a far greater influence on our mood and life experiences than many might acknowledge. The insidious nature of these influences underscores a pressing need for awareness and intervention in how technology is designed and deployed.

As technological advancements propel the economy to greater heights of efficiency, we inadvertently find ourselves navigating an increasingly complex landscape. This metaphorical ascent into the hills and mountains of competency leaves us on narrower, more crowded terrains, burdened further by the inefficiencies of institutional and governmental systems. It's my hope that the insights shared will encourage you to actively shape your surroundings, leveraging them for personal gain and well-being.

Consider the tranquil environments we instinctively seek for optimal productivity: a favored café, a quiet nook in a library, or a solitary cabin in nature. When these sanctuaries are out of reach, we often turn to digital forms of escape, such as music through earbuds or headphones, to craft a personal oasis from the chaos around us.

With the emergence of AR, VR, and MR, we're afforded unprecedented opportunities to curate environments that not only enhance our productivity but also enrich our lives in meaningful ways. While many of us may lack the means to transform our physical spaces dramatically, these technologies offer potent alternatives for personal and professional growth.

It's important to remember, however, that the ultimate goal is not to retreat indefinitely into these virtual worlds. Instead, AR and VR should be embraced as tools to facilitate focused, deep work—enabling us to tackle tasks that are crucial to our career advancement and personal satisfaction. These technologies serve as a bridge to achieving a sense of accomplishment, connection, and mastery over our work.

In the next chapter, we'll delve into the practical applications of designing such enriching virtual spaces, offering a roadmap for leveraging AR and VR technologies to create environments that support and amplify our goals and aspirations.

6

THE ROADMAP TO LEVERAGING AR AND VR TECHNOLOGIES

In our previous chapter, we delved into our environments' profound impact on our behaviors, performance, and emotions, underpinned by both theory and real-life instances. This understanding is crucial to construct a fresh approach towards the way we will go to work. In this new chapter, our focus shifts to crafting work environments that set you up for success in areas you value the most, be it your profession or career endeavors, family relationships, or personal well-being. Before we dive into that, let's first look at an essential aspect of this innovative work approach: strategic allotment of your time and energy.

Strategic Time and Energy Allocation

My typical day revolves around three significant areas of focus that govern my time, energy, and priority allocation. This concept of time management isn't new, but as you'll see, this method, in addition to your strategies, promises to be game-changing. There's no hard and fast rule about how many areas to focus on. I recommend playing it smart and simple by following the 'rule of threes,' which will soon unfold before you.

Aligning Vision and Values

The goal here is to help you structure your time so that your vision and values are perfectly in sync with your work environments, which are designed to draw from you the best of digital technologies, innate distinctly human capabilities, and a combination of both. Even those with highly structured jobs can adopt this approach with some pragmatic planning. This method prompts you to re-evaluate your core interests and skills and understand the pattern of your energy levels throughout the day.

Optimizing Work Focus

Harness Your Peak Performance Times

As a morning person, I have designed a focus area around tasks that are very important to my goals, and that demand intense concentration, as that's when I perform my best. I leverage VR's immersive environment in this 'work' focus area to make consistent progress in task-oriented aspects of your work and finances. The aim here is to optimize the factors in our external world we can control. This translates into aligning your time with your physical and mental energy cycles and harnessing digital technology to meet your work demands efficiently.

The Role of VR in Enhancing Focus

What makes VR technology truly remarkable is its ability to create a powerful sense of presence—the feeling of being genuinely "there" in a virtual environment. This heightened sense of reality sharpens focus and attention to detail because the brain perceives the experience as real. By fully engaging multiple senses—vision, hearing, and even touch through haptic feedback—VR immerses us in a way that naturally minimizes external distractions, making it easier to concentrate deeply on the task at hand.

In my everyday experience of working from home, distractions are both frequent and diverse—whether it's the buzz of my phone, the lure of the kitchen, or the temptation of a quick snack. To maintain focus during dedicated work sessions, I recommend turning off your phone and disabling social media apps. Additionally, try to create a sense of "virtual isolation," setting clear boundaries that minimize or eliminate distractions, allowing you to cultivate an environment that's truly optimized for concentration.

I find it valuable that VR can make routine or monotonous tasks more engaging by presenting them in novel and interactive ways. For example, I enjoy reviewing our financial results, often pages of boring detail, while sitting in the "immersed" environment called "Space Station," where I can simply look up and see planet Earth slowly revolving above me. This heightened engagement is somehow comforting and can increase motivation and focus.

As somewhat of a "quant," I love to work with data and results, and VR applications can more effectively incorporate tracking and feedback loops. This feedback, typically in the form of video and data, can help me improve and track my progress in those aspects of my work that need improvement. For me, these are around running a meeting and a group presentation.

Using the app Virtualspeech[1], I can practice and improve my speech or meeting presentations in brief, focused sessions in VR. Instant feedback can encourage a focused and continuous loop of practice and improvement.

When in VR, I also like to physically be isolated from their real environment (e.g., using headphones and headsets that block out external sights and sounds). This encapsulation can help block out interruptions and foster a deep focus.

During this brief, intense session, you'll be able to stay focused more effectively and take full advantage of the digital and AI tools to access the unlimited data that is available. These tools help us predict scenarios, better understand patterns, and tackle repetitive processes more effectively.

There is also the remarkable personal connection and virtual collaboration one can enjoy with VR, which is not available in any other medium. Connecting with an industry expert in Italy or Korea is now done at a far lower cost and with a high degree of personal connections in a way you may never have been able to prior to VR.

Many of us can easily get carried away with all the advantages of the VR environment, which is why I intentionally created an area of focus that includes our family, community, and well-being.

By intentionally structuring your day, you can deliberately make the time to spend with friends, family, and your community. No longer trying to juggle work and family, you now have a section of your day in which you leverage your uniquely human capabilities and our deep emotional range of love and forgiveness, contribution, personal touch, feel, and physical connection, as well as partnership and community.

Prioritizing Relationships and Wellbeing

In this area of focus, which I call "Relationships," you rely on and maximize your five senses and spend as much time physically together with those who matter most. During this time, there is minimal or no AR/VR usage or any activities that don't rely on these emotional strengths. It is also during this time that you exercise and focus on physical and mental well-being.

Embracing Creativity and Play

Leverage Creativity with AR/VR

Thirdly, there is the area of creativity, play, and collaboration with AR and VR that I call "Connection." Here, you leverage your creative, collaborative, and leadership strengths and gain motivation from the experiences of mastery, autonomy, and connection evoked in this area. In this area of focus, you participate in virtual meetings, coaching, mentoring, and collaboration with your team.

"What-If" Scenarios

Exploring "what-if" scenarios, especially in the realm of building services, proves highly effective in illustrating the intricate energy performance of entire building structures. Personally, I find no replacement for the experience of observing, alongside the architect and consulting engineer, how a building performs under various conditions. This collaborative approach allows us to grasp the nuances of building performance in response to different variables.

Innovating With AR/VR in Design

Similarly, leveraging augmented reality (AR) and virtual reality (VR) to swiftly visualize "what-if" scenarios in digital product design yields significant benefits. These technologies offer a dynamic platform for rapidly conceptualizing and evaluating different scenarios, enhancing our ability to iterate and innovate in the design process.

It is also in this area of focus, connection, in which you play... You give yourself the gift of mental stimulation and psychological well-being, and you play your favorite video game, a few sets of virtual tennis, or participate in some game or activity in the metaverse. While we will dig into this aspect more in chapter 9, there is compelling evidence that "playing" and participating in some of the metaverse games, in fact, supports and builds psychological health. The work and play you engage with here requires rapid shifting, a short burst of focus, and active listening. It also leverages the AR's ability to build upon an idea or a design you're working on.

Back to the Future

Immersive Experience in VR

After wearing what looks like sunglasses, you hop on a well-cushioned treadmill and go for a brisk walk. This magically transports you to the ESport^2 environment. As you begin your brisk walk, the landscape unfolds before your eyes. You're not just playing a game; you're living it. The sights, sounds, and sensations are so vivid that you feel a strong sense of presence as if walking alongside athletes in a real-world arena. This virtual world gives you a panoramic view reminiscent of what Alex experienced during his climb, with breathtaking vistas stretching into the distance. The horizon is full of life, activity, and excitement, drawing you deeper into the experience. Every detail is carefully rendered, from the texture of the virtual ground beneath your feet to the distant mountain ranges that seem just within reach.

This environment, besides being visually captivating, engages your whole body. The treadmill beneath you adjusts to match the incline or pace of your walk, providing a seamless physical interaction with the virtual space. As you walk faster, the scenery rushes by, making you feel like you're trekking through dynamic, challenging terrain. Your movements control your perspective, allowing you to look around, explore, and take in the environment at your own pace.

The Realism of Virtual Environments

It's truly astonishing to witness the breadth and lifelike realism offered by existing virtual environments, readily accessible at no cost, particularly within the Meta App called Immersed. Alongside this technological marvel, a relatively recent yet impactful psychological theory known as Stress Reduction Theory (SDT) underscores the profound influence of different environments on our moods and mindset. This theory draws from an interdisciplinary realm encompassing psychology, environmental psychology, neuroscience, and even architecture.

Understanding Biophilia

Central to this area of study is the concept of biophilia, stemming from the Greek words "bios," meaning life, and "philos," meaning love or attraction. Initially introduced by psychoanalyst Erich Fromm in the mid-20th century, biophilia gained widespread recognition through biologist Edward O. Wilson's seminal work "Biophilia," published in 1984[3]. Biophilia posits that humans are inclined to seek connections with nature and other life forms, a trait believed to be ingrained in our evolutionary history as hunter-gatherers.

This evolutionary perspective illuminates Alex's serene experience, suggesting that his sense of peace amidst open vistas and stone walls harkens back to an environment deemed safe from predators.

The concept of biophilia has transcended disciplinary boundaries, permeating fields such as psychology, architecture, urban planning, and environmentalism. Its core tenet underscores the importance of integrating nature into our built environments to enhance well-being and foster sustainability and ecological harmony.

The Therapeutic Power of Nature

The power of nature's awesome beauty ought not to be underestimated. Studies have proven that the simple act of beholding open landscapes, lush greenery, and serene bodies of water greatly diminishes stress levels and elevates mood[4]. This visual intake of natural scenes stimulates a healing process within our brains, effectively curbing mental exhaustion and promoting a sense of tranquility.

Attention Restoration Theory (ART)[5]

As proposed by the Attention Restoration Theory (ART), soft fascinations are inherent to natural environments. These captivate our senses gently, fostering the regeneration of our cognitive system, which in turn amplifies mood and cognitive function. The benefits don't stop there—physical health also gets a boost. Take, for instance, hospital patients with a room view of nature. They recuperate at a faster pace and require less pain relief than those lacking such views.[6]

Biophilia and Productivity

By introducing the concept of 'biophilia,' we underline our surroundings' profound influence on our lives, including our productivity and motivation levels. This means that by deliberately and pragmatically adding natural elements to our environment, we can harness its therapeutic potential to our advantage.

The Future of Environmental Design

Next, we're going to look at another constituent that you can use in the design of your environment. Because of VR/AR, you have total control over this powerful element.

Before we go there, we will touch on AI in the next section and in the coming chapter, and I wanted to share what I mean by AI. I use the term AI without any implication of AI intelligence or the "so-called singularity." Frankly, you shouldn't necessarily listen to me, or most people, when it comes to their opinions of AI, but in the words of Jardon Lanier, one of the recognized founders of AI and Time Magazine's top 100 intellectuals of our time, among many other accolades.

I'll paraphrase, but Jaron said in an interview with physicist Brian Green in a World Science PodCast[7] when asked about the potential destruction of mankind at the hands of AI:

> *"AI is just another technology. What is to be feared is man and what he will do with it. Look, we have had technology that will end our existence on the planet for decades, and we haven't done it. Why will this be different?"*

Masterpieces in Motion: BMWs, Pianos, and the Art of Creating Your Environment

Let's explore the art of crafting environments that cultivate success and well-being. We now understand the profound impact nature can have on our well-being and productivity. One of your tasks ahead is identifying the precise natural scenes that energize you the most. We will explore pioneering software that will help you do just that.

However, there's another dimension to engineering your environment that we've been manipulating without much thought. It's about understanding and tailoring this element to serve your best interests, regardless of where you are. To understand this better, we'll draw insights from individuals who mastered the craft of their environments for maximum productivity and creativity.

Steve Jobs: Inspiration through Craftsmanship

Steve Jobs, renowned for his relentless pursuit of aesthetic and functional excellence in his products, found inspiration in diverse places. This included a deep admiration for the craftsmanship and design of BMW motorcycles and Bösendorfer pianos. Walter Isaacson, Jobs's friend and biographer, shared how Jobs saw BMW's engineering and design brilliance as the apex of practical beauty and technical prowess.

During his early days at Apple, Jobs would ride his BMW to work, helmetless, of course, and park it in the Apple lobby. This was no whimsical act but a deliberate move to let his team be in the presence of an object that embodied the harmonious coexistence of design and engineering.

Equally inspiring for Jobs was the Bösendorfer piano, acclaimed for its unmatched sound quality and exquisite craftsmanship. Bösendorfer, one of the oldest piano makers, is a testament to traditional craftsmanship and the pursuit of perfection. Jobs held these values close to his heart.

By showcasing these objects in the lobby, Jobs aimed to set the tone for Apple's working environment. He sought to encourage his team by immersing them in a space that drew out excellence in craftsmanship and design. Jobs's message was unambiguous: Apple products must emulate the craftsmanship, finesse, and aesthetic appeal of his BMW motorcycle and the Bösendorfer piano. In doing so, he believed that Apple could produce technology that was not just cutting-edge but also possessed the ability to connect emotionally with its users in the same way that a finely crafted musical instrument could stir its audience.

Throughout history, design has been pivotal in shaping religious and cultural experiences. From ancient temples to modern cathedrals, design has been a powerful tool for conveying spiritual meaning and invoking awe. Sacred spaces, created by the Egyptians, Greeks, Hindus, and Christians, were meticulously designed to inspire reverence, foster community, and connect worshipers with the divine. The intention behind these spaces was to elevate the human spirit, guiding individuals to reflect on larger truths, mysteries, and shared beliefs.

The architecture and layout of religious buildings often followed symbolic patterns designed to direct attention toward key focal points such as altars, shrines, or domes. This focus on design was not merely aesthetic; it was deeply functional, encouraging spiritual contemplation, unity, and devotion. Gothic cathedrals, for example, with their towering spires and stained-glass windows, were designed to convey the grandeur and omnipotence of God. The verticality of these structures was a visual metaphor for the human journey toward heaven, while the intricate details of religious iconography spoke to the complexity of the divine.

Likewise, tribal communities used design to solidify their identity and beliefs. Totems, masks, and communal spaces were often designed with spiritual significance, used to tell stories, record history, and represent ancestral connections. These design elements beautified the environment, strengthened cultural bonds, and created a shared experience of belonging.

The strategic use of materials, colors, light, and space was central to religious and tribal design traditions. Gold and precious stones symbolized divinity and eternity, while light was often used as a metaphor for spiritual enlightenment. In Islamic architecture, for instance, intricate geometric patterns and calligraphy express the infinite nature of God while avoiding any depiction of human forms, keeping the focus on spiritual transcendence rather than material existence.

Jobs's approach to design at Apple can be seen as drawing from these timeless traditions. Just as religious and tribal leaders used design to shape mindsets and reinforce communal values, Jobs employed design in Apple's spaces and products to inspire innovation and cultivate a shared sense of purpose. His emphasis on crafting environments that stimulate creativity and excellence parallels how religious spaces were crafted to evoke a sense of wonder and transcendence.

In much the same way that sacred spaces guided people's thoughts toward the divine, Jobs believed that beautifully designed objects could inspire his team to think differently and create products that transcended their function. Apple's products, like religious artifacts, were designed to be more than utilitarian—they were intended to be meaningful, deeply resonant, and capable of evoking emotional responses from users. Just as ancient religious designs sought to connect humanity with the divine, Apple's design philosophy aimed to connect people with technology in intuitive, human, and spiritual ways.

This philosophy became a cornerstone of Apple's brand message, driving the company to pursue excellence in design and engineering. The influence of these principles is evident in the meticulous attention to detail, the choice of materials, and the integration of form and function in Apple products, from the Macintosh computers to the iPhone.

So, as you curate your surroundings, seek out those objects that speak to your soul, ignite your imagination, and beckon you to strive for greatness. These icons will inspire you to reach new heights, push boundaries, and, with just a glance, transport you to a realm of inspiration and possibility—a realm uniquely yours, akin to Steve Jobs' BMW or Bösendorfer piano.

Much like Jobs' iconic objects, your chosen items should evoke a sense of purpose and aspiration. They should constantly remind you of your journey, values, and vision for the future. Whether it's a meticulously crafted piece of furniture, a cherished work of art, or a symbol of achievement, these objects have the ability to elevate your environment and mindset.

For me, it is the kayak that hangs in my cottage on Moose Lake[8], as well as the digital kayak I take with me and place in work and leisure environments. My Dad crafted this kayak, and to me, it personifies his attention to and love of craftsmanship, his rugged spirit, and his generous heart.

Apple has continued to embrace this fundamental idea that the environment and icons in it influence its employees. Under Tim Cook's leadership, Apple strongly emphasizes bringing the outside in. Apple Park has over 9,000 trees planted on the campus. The campus's design, with its large glass panels, allows for abundant natural light and offers expansive views of the surrounding landscape, blurring the boundaries between indoors and outdoors.

Vincent Van Gogh: Painting En Plein Air

Van Gogh was known for his love of painting "en plein air" outdoors. This allowed him to immerse himself in the natural world and capture its beauty and vitality firsthand. He often set up his easel outdoors, whether in the countryside, along the coast, or in bustling city streets, to paint landscapes, seascapes, and scenes of everyday life.

Painting en plein air offered van Gogh a sense of immediacy and spontaneity in his work, as he responded to the changing light, weather, and atmosphere in real-time. It allowed him to capture the nuances of color, texture, and form observed directly from nature, resulting in vibrant, dynamic paintings infused with a sense of life and energy.

For Van Gogh, painting en plein air was a practical technique and a philosophical approach to art. It enabled him to tap into that ancient innate connection, the biophilia, and have a direct and intimate connection with the natural world, fostering a deep appreciation for its beauty and majesty. By painting outdoors, he sought to capture the essence of his surroundings and convey the emotional and spiritual significance of the landscapes he encountered.

Biographers of Van Gogh[9] go to some length to explain that paint brushes were more than mere tools; they were extensions of his artistic vision and innermost thoughts. The paintbrushes, always strewn around his studio and apartments, were van Gogh's reminder of his unwavering commitment to his craft and his relentless pursuit of artistic excellence, his BMW, piano, or kayak.

Jeremy Bailenson: Exploring VR's Potential

Jeremy Bailenson looks like the guy who just changed the oil in my truck at Jiffy Lube. Wearing a black tee shirt, jeans, and long, shaggy hair tucked behind his ears, he looks completely out of place on the TEDx stage. After about 5 seconds, you realize he is the real thing. After all, he is the founding director of Stanford University's Virtual Human Interaction Lab and has a list of titles, including being a Senior Fellow at the Woods Institute for the Environment. In addition to his ultra-casual presentation, you realize this guy is someone who can bring important insights to working in AR/VR. Not only does he have a Ph.D. in cognitive psychology from Northwestern University, but he spent four years at the University of California, Santa Barbara, as a Post-Doctoral Fellow, also learning every component in detail, taking apart the AR/VR technology and putting them back together while using them for his research.

Back in 2011, I stumbled upon his book *Infinite Reality*, authored by him and Professor Jim Blascovich. This book rapidly became my compass, guiding me to work smarter, not harder. The book delves into the transformative potential of Virtual Reality (VR) and its considerable effects on our well-being, explicitly showcasing how digitally constructed nature influences our psychological state. This captivating exploration formed the basis of my interest in AR/VR.

In their well-researched book, Bailenson and Blascovich illuminate VR's unique capability to render immersive natural environments, leading to experiences that can positively enhance our psychological and emotional states. They back these findings with substantial data, including FMRI results and various objective physiological findings like blood tests, demonstrating the profound therapeutic benefits of VR exposure. Imagine reducing stress, anxiety, and depression just by strolling through virtual woods, mountains, or beaches.

So, my fellow engineers and creatives, regardless of your prior interest or preference for nature in your workspace, adding a touch of it will inevitably yield positive results. It could be a crucial element in the work environment you create. To lend a more scientific angle, and for those who value research-backed data, Professor Sir Cary Cooper conducted a study in 2015 involving 7,600 office employees from 16 different nations. His findings revealed that a design incorporating elements of nature significantly boosts workers' productivity, creativity, and overall well-being.

When we intersect these findings with Bailenson's[10] work, we uncover an exciting array of tools for designing and engineering our environments. That's precisely what we'll delve into in the upcoming chapter.

7

THE POWER OF NATURE

Alex grew up on the edge of a small but bustling city nestled at the foot of towering emerald peaks. With his parents' separation years ago when he was just eight years old, Alex had often found himself adrift in a sea of emotional unrest, compounded by the relentless challenges to fit in at school, often the subject of teasing. Small for his age and often lost in thought, Alex was easy prey for the bullies who couldn't see beyond the small physical appearance to the mountainous spirit within.

School was a daily trial, a trek through a barren landscape of incomprehensible words and figures. Letters and numbers jumbled up before Alex's eyes like cryptic code, thwarting his efforts to learn and be part of the crowd. The bullies, like invisible vultures circling above, could strike at any time.

The city, with its honking cars and endless concrete, suffocated him, a world away from the tranquility and majestic beauty of the mountains he so loved. Perhaps it was the fresh breeze, whispering through the leaves, or the stoic silence of the rocky outcrops that brought solace to Alex's restless spirit. Nature's grand theater, just outside his bedroom window, performed a spectacle of awe that captivated his soul, providing the freedoms he yearned for in his caged existence.

Despair gripped Alex on a suffocating afternoon as he sat trapped in a hot, smelly car with his unhappy and unstable mother, with her frustrations with traffic and life seemingly directed at him. The limitations of this city pressed on him from all sides; the steel gray of the buildings resembled bars he could not bend. A crushing weight compressed his chest as he contemplated the ultimate escape that spelled a finality no child should have to consider.

The library was no place for him, but essentially free child care for his stressed-out Mom. It was not at all uncommon for Alex to climb the library shelves, but today he found something called a Tyco View-Master. Dusty and lodged behind a heavy book on the top shelf, he thought it was a cheap pair of binoculars, but after looking into them, what was unveiled before him was awe unfolding—a portal to a wider world. A stunning mountain vista leaped into view, and Alex was there, engulfed in beauty too raw, too wondrous to be contained within the bones of a library building.

It wasn't some ethereal whisper this time, but the rugged silence of the mountains that spoke to him. Each jagged peak and weathered rock seemed to tell tales of stability and resilience, etched into the very landscape. In that moment of awe, Alex saw and felt a different future for himself.

His connection with the mountains grew deeper as he saw his own struggles mirrored in their towering presence. Amidst the raw embrace of nature, Alex found solace and strength. Here, there was no judgment, just the unyielding acceptance of the elements.

Just being in the same environment, be it real or virtual, one can't help but feel the power of the sheer magnitude of nature. Every rugged contour and jagged edge seems to resonate with our very essence, tapping into an innate understanding of the patient yet reliable forces that have meticulously crafted and molded the landscape.

Yet, it was through the View-Master that he could gaze down from the peak, wondering what he would look like from the perspective of someone at this vantage. In that moment of clarity, he felt small, insignificant, even, yet strangely liberated from the chaos that surrounded him in the city.

What Alex felt was a textbook experience of awe, the unique emotion that Dacher Keltner, a psychologist at the University of California, Berkeley, and the author of *Awe: The New Science of Everyday Wonder and How It Can Transform Your Life,*[1] defines as the "feeling of being in the presence of something vast that transcends your current understanding of the world." In fact, the "overview effect"— envisioning yourself or the world from a great distance—is one of the most reliable ways to evoke awe.

Slowly at first, his life pointed in a new direction, and with every new peak, ledge, or face he summited, he became a teacher, mentoring him toward clarity and determination. Nature molded him, not with grand gestures, but with quiet persistence, like the wind shaping a canyon. The bullies still lurked, but their taunts lost their sting. The awe he felt among the peaks fueled his determination, instilling a newfound confidence in himself and his craft.

Alex's story isn't just about climbing —it's about the power of nature. Through his journey, we will continue to learn to appreciate life's grandeur and find strength in its vastness. While it was the awe and majesty of the mountains that inspired and encouraged Alex, for some of us it is the vastness of the Arabian deserts or the beauty of peaceful sunset.

The core inspiration behind this story rests on the evolving body of evidence that suggests profound experiences—particularly those evoked by the enormity and beauty of nature—can indeed shape our emotional well-being and outlook on life.

In their seminal paper[2], psychologists Dacher Keltner and Jonathan Haidt proposed the concept of "awe" as an emotion characterized by feelings of vastness, a need for accommodation, and a sense of smallness in the face of something greater than oneself.

Their research suggests that experiencing awe can lead to a range of positive outcomes, including increased feelings of well-being, prosocial behavior, and a greater sense of purpose in life.

These studies represent just one of a growing body of research exploring the effects of awe on psychological health and motivation. Overall, the findings suggest that experiencing awe can have profound effects on various aspects of well-being, including happiness, life satisfaction, prosocial behavior, and motivation.

Now, why is this important to you in a book about going to work in the era of AR/VR/XR?

Several studies have explored how VR, in particular, can also evoke feelings of awe by providing immersive experiences that simulate vast and awe-inspiring environments[3]. For example, virtual simulations of natural wonders such as the Grand Canyon or Northern Lights, or even fictional environments like outer space or fantastical landscapes, can elicit feelings of awe in users.

There are now dozens of such studies which investigate the potential of VR to induce awe and in almost every case participants reported significantly higher levels of awe after experiencing VR compared to traditional 2D media. The immersive nature of VR allowed participants to feel more present in the simulated environment, enhancing their emotional responses.

Reflecting on this, it appears in some way that the experiences conjured by Steve Jobs' BMW or piano might actually serve as symbolic surrogates of the awe of the mountains that beckon us with a soft whisper of possibility—an example and tantalizing invitation to challenge the limits of what's possible and to reach for the sky.

Recognizing the pressing need for a renewed approach to our daily work routines, it's abundantly clear that the current standard falls far short of nurturing our well-being and personal fulfillment.

In the forthcoming chapters, this book is set to challenge the very foundations of traditional "going to work," offering a roadmap that transcends the mundane to embrace the extraordinary. It's a call to arms for investing our time wisely in both work and life, advocating for purposeful living and intelligent strategies tailored to each individual's unique journey.

This isn't just transformational mumbo-jumbo; it's a meticulously researched endeavor grounded in deliberate action. As I wrote these words, I found sanctuary in the serenity of a cabin by Moose Lake—a humble home that speaks to my soul. Day in and day out, I turn to virtual reality (VR) to navigate my tasks, stay fit, and be connected to others, especially when the elements conspire against outdoor pursuits. In this digital realm, I've found not just a refuge, but a remedy for the soul-sucking grip of traffic, mindless screen time scrolling, or other such bullshit.

In addition, including VR work sessions will provide the added effect of bringing intentionality to your day - and with it the profound impact of the tools available.

Drawing inspiration from the transformative evolution of dating apps, where more people now, in 2024, meet their mates online than in any other place, we witness a seismic shift in the dynamics of human connection. Where once physical appearance reigned supreme, now the spotlight shines on shared interests and values, facilitating deeper and more meaningful connections.

With the emergence of AR/VR/MR, we intentionally transcend the limitations of physical boundaries, tapping into what is our most powerful primal feelings and forging bonds untainted by biases and prejudices. It will seem odd and stupid even to spend up to a third of your day in traffic.

In attempting to create a whole new way to go to work, I feel it is fair for me to acknowledge that the way we go to work now is certainly not anything that produces well-being or positive feelings. The purpose of this book is to disrupt the legacy approach to "going to work" and identify the best way to spend your time working and living a life. I like to think it is an inclusive way to live intentionally, looking for practical and intelligent ways to work and live that work for you.

That works in that it is intentional and draws upon research. Personally, in writing this book, I have moved my home to a cabin on Moose Lake, not exactly Walden Pond, but pretty damn nice. I use VR daily to get my work done, to exercise when the weather does not permit, and to engage in a host of social and personal learning. In fact, exercising in VR encourages me to reproduce those experiences outside. It is the opposite of what TV and binge-watching did to me in every era before.

There's certainly no shortage of criticism of the seemingly "unnatural" or "non-human" aspect of the upcoming tech-driven approach, nor its utility beyond the "cool" factor. I, however, continue to advocate for the profound benefits this particular technology brings. One aspect of VR technology that has made a remarkable difference for me is that of learning and training. In our industry, we are the intersection of new technologies and existing building systems. It is imperative to stay up to date with the new products and technology.

Like Alex, I too have struggled with some aspects of learning, as I often have a difficult time translating and assembling the letters into letter into words, and then words into the right order, particularly when I'm reading aloud. As an author, this is highly stressful. Also, I thought perhaps I had AHDH or some other malady, which challenged my ability to stay focused on a task.

Today, because of the rapidly rising tide of technology, more kids and even business people like me have the opportunity to use VR/AR/XR to learn at their own pace and in a way designed to address learning limitations. With access to this type of training, we can all avoid the soul-crushing experience of public humiliation because they're unable to read. I cannot think that Alex's trials and decisions were a result of an untreated learning limitation. An issue I have also struggled with is social anxiety, and just like with learning difficulties, there are now great online VR tools that help address this debilitating phobia.

In the next chapter, we'll sketch out in detail what it is you can do and how you plan your day, and offer some current information about software and hardware you may enjoy.

8

THE CROSSROAD

Minneapolis was frozen solid in December when I moved from Dubai to our corporate headquarters. That day is etched in my memory... I went to the hotel gym, gazed out at the grey snow flurries whipping through the downtown canyons of office buildings, and wondered if this was truly a promotion.

Another vivid memory: often wishing for a chance to do things over.

I began my usual warm-ups, but the inviting setup of the squat rack tempted me to perform some light squats to engage my larger muscles and prepare my body for the workout.

It happened during the second or third squat—an exercise in which a barbell rests on your shoulders behind your neck, and you keep your back fairly straight as you bend your knees. There was no snap or crack, just a strange sensation like water pouring over my right hip and the front of my right leg. Puzzled, I checked for water, then reset for another squat when a sharp, ripping pain struck my lower back... I knew immediately something was seriously wrong.

Struggling to maintain composure, I tried to walk it off, but the pain soon became unbearable. I had never fainted before, yet the intensity of the pain had me seeing streaks of light, like shooting stars, at the edge of my vision.

In the days that followed, I stubbornly pushed through the pain to meet my professional obligations, even using crutches. My determination didn't wane until it was clear I wasn't improving.

A shift in perspective came during a visit to the urgent care clinic. After a couple of quick knocks, a young, five-foot-tall doctor who looked like she could still be in high school burst into the room. She was a remarkably capable physician whose expertise quickly dispelled any preconceived notions about her age or stature. With a stern gaze, she directed me to the x-ray images on the towering monitors, showing various angles of my damaged lower back.

"You have a serious injury, Mr. Dorey, and should not be walking around," she declared with clinical precision. "You need to see a neurosurgeon immediately."

This diagnosis highlighted a long-standing battle with low back issues, dating back to my early teens. A previous fracture of the transverse process on L-4 had caused me chronic pain since I was around twelve or thirteen.

Years later, as a thirty-something, doctors recommended a mechanical fusion—a complex procedure involving both orthopedic and neurosurgeons. For eight hours, they meticulously fused two vertebrae with titanium hardware, stabilizing my spine and alleviating years of discomfort. This solution was meant to last 10-20 years; remarkably, it held for 30. Because the fusion shifted stress along the plate to the vertebrae ends, it eventually led to a crushing and compressing of my L-5 vertebrae.

Within days, I saw a neurosurgeon. His stark, large waiting room was completely full.

The surgery was harrowing—there's no way to sugarcoat that. The recovery was slow, painful, and emotionally taxing for months. Even after the surgery, the extent of damage to my spinal cord was uncertain, though we all hoped for a 100% recovery. However, after 18 months of physical therapy, human growth hormone therapy, and exploring every possible avenue, I was left with almost no plantar flexion in my right foot.

Plantar flexion is the ability of the muscles to push down, as when stepping forward in a normal stride or pressing down on a gas pedal. With almost none remaining, I now have a limp—a painful and humiliating reminder of my ordeal with each step I take.

The actual incident isn't what causes me the most anguish; it's the poor decisions I made afterward that could have been avoided. Yet, I know I'm not the only one who has felt the compulsion to "go to work" at all costs.

We've made going to work a demonstration of our commitment and worth, but as I can attest, had I been given the opportunity to work from home, things might have been different.

Reflecting on that fateful moment in the gym, I realized with a pang of regret the unwitting role I had played in my own downfall.

This realization brought to light two key reasons why this particular episode and injury are central themes in a book about transforming our approach to work.

Firstly, the availability of remote work options, particularly with advancements in VR and AR technology, might have prevented further damage to my spinal cord, sparing me from a permanent limp. Moreover, emerging research into pain management using VR/AR is proving promising, highlighting the potential of technology to improve physical well-being in the workspace.

Secondly, there's a pervasive culture in many global corporations that equates constant work with honor and worth. This mindset insists that a life dedicated to work, often at the expense of physical health, is virtuous. It was this mindset that influenced my poor decisions after the injury.

About two years after the surgery, a combination of factors led me into a downward spiral, both physically and emotionally. I was at the end of my rope, figuratively speaking, and needed to heal or risk sinking further into the mire of victimhood and a lifestyle dependent on opioid pain medications and increasing amounts of single malt scotch.

During that critical period, I mustered the courage to seek help. I checked into a small private rehab center, committing to a month of focused mental and physical health rehabilitation—a decision I remain proud of ten years later.

Following this transformative experience, I found myself at a crossroads. It was not just an opportunity to rebuild but to reconnect with the dreams and aspirations that once fueled my ambition. With renewed clarity and a resolute desire to recapture what I had lost, I embarked on a journey of self-reconstruction.

During this time, I discovered the value of stepping back. I learned that the world doesn't pause when I do—that it continues to turn, even without my constant vigilance over every CNN news cycle. This realization was liberating, allowing me to focus on nurturing my mind and body without the guilt of not "going to work."

I decided to make a significant change and relocated to Charlottesville, VA—a picturesque town steeped in history and home to Thomas Jefferson and the university he founded, UVA. Having worked nearby early in my corporate career, I was familiar with the area and felt a deep, almost gravitational pull towards it. Although I didn't fully understand it at the time, I believe I was drawn to the solace offered by the rolling hills of the Shenandoah Valley. They seemed to cocoon me, shielding me from the world's turmoil and creating a sanctuary where I could heal and grow.

Walking became a cornerstone of my daily routine. What began as a challenging four-minute venture—two minutes out and two minutes back—gradually evolved. After about six or seven months, I extended my walks outdoors and complemented them with indoor sessions. I began using VR technology and an elliptical trainer to create a diverse, immersive experience that lasted around forty minutes each day. This blend of real and virtual landscapes not only enhanced my physical stamina but also provided a mental escape, aiding my overall recovery and strengthening my resolve to move forward.

It was during this time that I allowed my energy level and mental alertness to guide the structure of my day. I did not set out to develop a system; I simply tried to "ride the horse in the direction it wanted to go," an important lesson from my grandfather, Jacob Joseph Dorey.

Howard Roark - Creative, Architect, Engineer

Ayn Rand's *The Fountainhead* explores the struggle for individualism in a conformist society. The plot centers on Howard Roark, a no-Bullshit young architect who battles against traditional standards and refuses to be bound by societal expectations. Roark's journey is important in the creation of a whole new way to work.

In his iconic courtroom speech, Roark declares:

> *"I do not recognize anyone's right to one minute of my life. Nor to any part of my energy, nor to any achievement of mine. The creator lives for his work. He needs no other men. His primary goal is within himself."*

These words compel us to embrace individuality and vision, ensuring that the collective's Bullshit never drowns our inner voice.

In the world of VR and AR technologies, we are more than participants—we are architects, creators, and engineers, shaping our work environments to reflect our unique visions. Like Roark, our primary drive comes from within.

This book—and the very idea of *A Whole New Way to Work*—challenges us to embrace these emerging technologies and ideas without being swayed by the misinformation that often clouds groundbreaking advancements. Rather than conforming to a collective mold, we should celebrate individuality, foster innovation, and express our creativity.

At its core, *A Whole New Way to Work* envisions a world where we are not confined by convention or misconceptions but empowered by our own ingenuity. It invites us to step beyond limitations and boldly explore the future of VR.

Remember, the first step is yours to take.

VR in Building Systems

Gone are the days of merely replicating buildings from the past by plastering Roman columns on any structure. With his forward-thinking vision and commitment to originality, Roark would have been a VR advocate, allowing him to reimagine spaces in real time, exploring innovative solutions without the constraints of the physical world.

In this new era, lifestyle and workspaces will be seamlessly integrated. Meetings with clients will soon take on a new dimension as AR overlays superimpose proposed designs onto existing structures, allowing you and your team to visualize concepts while walking through them. VR simulations offer immersive walkthroughs of prospective installations, giving clients a firsthand experience of their future environment and fostering informed decision-making. This convergence of technology and creativity paves the way for a lifestyle where the boundaries between imagination and reality blur, embodying the spirit of Roark's architectural philosophy.

The impact of AR and VR extends far beyond marketing pitches and client consultations. These technologies are revolutionizing the way work is done—streamlining installation and troubleshooting by providing digital overlays that guide technicians through complex tasks, reducing errors, and improving efficiency.

My goal is to capture the essence of this profound transformation in how we perceive "going to work." By integrating AR and VR into our daily routines, we are not just reshaping work—we are eliminating the very need to *go* to work. It's like turning water into vapor; once the shift is complete, the original form ceases to exist. In this new reality, the notion of commuting to a physical workspace simply dissolves.

In this bold new era, engineers, creatives, and business leaders are not just adapting to change—they are pioneering it. They are sculpting their environments with the limitless potential of AR and VR. And as they embrace this challenge of discovery, one truth becomes evident: the only real constraints are those of imagination and courage—the same unyielding spirit exemplified by Roark.

The Structure of Your Day

Before we dive deeper, let's acknowledge that any structure we impose is rooted in our past experiences. While it's tempting to ponder the timeless question of "turtles all the way down,"[1] practicality demands a starting point.

In this pursuit, I find solace in the wisdom of one of the most influential industrial minds of the digital era, Dieter Rams. As the chief design officer of the iconic Braun Corporation, Rams championed the ethos of "Less is More," a philosophy that transcended consumer products to redefine office design principles.

This ethos resonates with the innovative spirit of individuals like Jonathan Ive, a protégé of Braun's, and the visionary behind Apple's minimalist designs. Their collective legacy challenges conventional notions of work, stripping away the bullshit to reveal a structure that aligns with our natural rhythms. What both of these iconic designers have done to digital products is pressing out against the wider environments of how and where we "go to work." In the vocabulary of earlier chapters, they removed the bullshit (traffic, endless meetings...) and, in fact, validated the design and structure of the Day, which I have found works best for me. One of simplicity and natural adaptability.

The core of this design philosophy stands for Benjamin Franklin, a man truly ahead of his time and a pioneer whose pragmatic approach to time management remains relevant today. Franklin's biographer, Walter Isaacson, meticulously documented his practice of dividing the Day into dedicated blocks of time for various pursuits. While not groundbreaking, this framework, rooted in natural areas of focus like work, study, and leisure, forms the cornerstone of my own approach.

To distill the essence of Dieter Rams' minimalist brilliance alongside Franklin's practical wisdom into actionable strategies, I propose a focus on three key areas:

1. Work
2. Connection/Relationships
3. Creativity/Collaboration/Play

These elements interplay dynamically, similar to how variables integrate in integral calculus. Unlike simple averages, which offer a broad, static value, integration accounts for the continuous accumulation of these small changes, furnishing a comprehensive view of motion or, in our case, energy level and motivation.

Embracing this concept of integral calculus in our daily planning, we recognize that not all segments of time yield the same productivity. Mornings, for instance, tend to be more productive for me. Thus, strategically choosing the optimal times for activities during your Day and week can significantly enhance your efficiency and effectiveness.

The first area, which we will call "Work," embodies deep focus, ideally flow and uninterrupted attention—an immersive experience facilitated by the advancements in VR technology. By harnessing VR's capabilities, we create an environment conducive to concentration, tapping into our peak cognitive abilities during morning hours. This focused session, lasting 45-90 minutes, is devoid of distractions, allowing for optimal productivity.

The second area of focus, "Connection/Relationships", lies outside of too much AR/VR technology. In this domain, we employ the unique and remarkable human-only capabilities of love, connection, and relationship.

While I'm not a digital minimalist, I do believe it's imperative to thoughtfully allocate time for our personal relationships in the design of our day. Even the new cult classic *Ready Player One* emphasizes the irreplaceable depth of real-life relationships and emotional connections, highlighting the significance of prioritizing human interaction in a technology-driven world.

The third area of focus encompasses "Creativity, Collaboration, and Play"—a space where both AR and VR unlock boundless opportunities for innovation. Central to this area of focus is the power of collaboration, facilitated by VR's ability to transcend geographical barriers. This convergence of minds in a virtual space fosters unparalleled rapid connection and synergy, laying the foundation for transformative partnerships. This area can be used for business or other pursuits.

While the potential of AR and VR is undeniable, today, in early 2024, existing collaboration tools still lag.

The 3-D Venn diagram below depicts the confluence of the three elements as they move through time, the fourth element. I like to think of the integration of the time element as using your "stock" of energy throughout the Day.

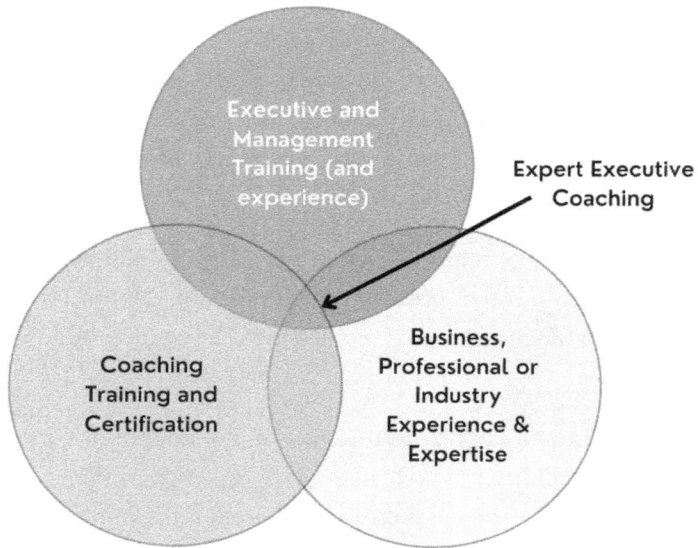

The Structure of Your Day in VR

With a simple connection to my MacBook Pro laptop[2], the internet, and the Quest 2 headset, I can create for myself a super productive setup. My initial and still go-to setup is a mirror of my computer, but now with three massive screens curving in a semi-circle floating in mid-air around my body, strategically located so I can see either the earth as I revolve around it in a cool spaceship, or get the best view of the lakes and valleys hundreds of feet below the Lakeview Lodge.

While the screen setup and ease of view and usage are productive, what truly captivates me is the visual of the Lakeview Lodge (rainy), in which I sit.

Picture this: I'm on a cozy couch in a huge, modern, yet rustic lodge setting. The 360-degree view out the window looks down upon lush green forests, serene lakes, rugged cliffs, and inviting beaches. It's as though you're perched atop the highest hill, soaking in the breathtaking panorama.

I often find myself returning to this "room" to do deep work, and it's not solely for its aesthetic appeal. The environment, complete with a gentle rain in the background, engages my senses. The vibrant greens, soothing blues, and earthy browns fill my visual field, instinctively melting away stress like nothing else I've tried.

In this serene setting, I notice a subtle shift within me—a deep inhalation followed by a prolonged exhalation, as if my body is releasing pent-up tension with each breath. This pronounced sighing is a visceral response, a natural rhythm that helps recalibrate my breathing patterns and wash away the stresses of the Day. It's a tangible reminder of the profound impact our surroundings can have on our well-being, harnessing the power of nature and technology to promote relaxation, focus, and productivity.

Flow and Leapfrogging

It's essential to understand why, decades after its introduction, prioritizing *flow* in the workplace is more relevant than ever. In the rapidly evolving landscape of modern technology, "technological leapfrogging" allows us to bypass traditional methods and dive straight into innovative solutions, much like how cell phone technology leapfrogs landlines in developing countries.

Traditionally, achieving a state of flow[3]—an intensely focused state of immersion and productivity—was often seen in extreme sports athletes, musicians, or monks, where the alignment of skill and challenge leads to transcendent experiences. However, with the rapid evolution of technology, VR has emerged as a groundbreaking tool that democratizes access to this coveted flow state.

The rapid advancements in VR technology exemplify technological leapfrogging by skipping over incremental improvements and revolutionizing how we interact with digital environments. VR immerses individuals in a controlled, distraction-free setting tailor-made for deep work. This environment is selected and designed to match your skills with the challenges at hand, mirroring the conditions that foster flow in extreme sports or creative performances.

If you've read a couple of non-fiction business or productivity books in the past decade, you're probably familiar with the concept of *flow*. It would be even more impressive if you could pronounce the name of the guy who originally wrote about it at the University of Chicago in the 1970s. Mihaly Csikszentmihalyi's work on flow and the subsequent avalanche of research have clarified the conditions necessary for entering this state and the experience itself. The interest in this research stems from the extraordinary nature of flow.

Flow is particularly relevant in the context of the next generation of work. We've all experienced it: pushing ourselves, free from self-consciousness and worry, losing track of time—like when working on a crossword puzzle or writing an emotionally important email.

In a VR setting, a programmer could be transported to a serene virtual office, free from the usual workplace interruptions, with customized difficulty levels in coding challenges that keep their skills sharply engaged. Similarly, writers might find themselves in a distraction-free virtual cabin, mirroring Thoreau's, with the sounds of nature enhancing their focus and creativity. This precise calibration of environment and challenge prime individuals for flow, a state previously reached serendipitously by athletes and artists through a perfect confluence of conditions.

Now, thanks to VR, we're not just stumbling upon these moments— we can create them!

This shift is monumental—what once required natural talent and extraordinary circumstances can now be systematically and repeatedly engineered. VR doesn't just mimic the real-world conditions necessary for flow; it enhances them, offering settings and scenarios far beyond the physical world's limitations.

Thus, as we embrace these rapid technological changes, we gain a new VR tool and a new paradigm for productivity and personal development. By leveraging VR, we're not merely keeping pace with technology; we're leapfrogging into a future where the elite state of flow is accessible to everyone, transforming how we work and how we will go to work into opportunities for profound satisfaction and achievement.

These findings highlight the broader application of VR in enhancing flow experiences[4]. VR's capacity to create engaging and interactive environments aligns with the flow principles, where you become fully absorbed. By simulating real-world challenges and offering immediate feedback, VR helps you achieve and maintain flow, enhancing Motivation and performance over time.

The research by K. Wong, C. Chan, and colleagues underscores VR's potential as a powerful tool for fostering Motivation, learning, and adaptive skills. Their pilot study explored VR technology's ability to facilitate flow states in occupational settings. Participants engaged in VR-based tasks designed to promote focus, challenge, and skill development. The results indicated that VR interventions effectively induced flow states characterized by heightened focus, intrinsic Motivation, and optimal performance, offering promising applications for enhancing productivity and well-being in the workplace.

The findings suggest promising applications of VR technology as we design a whole new way to work. By leveraging VR interventions, organizations can potentially enhance performance, well-being, and overall job satisfaction. VR-based training programs, simulations, and skill development activities offer opportunities for creating flow-inducing experiences at work.

Perhaps most important to me now is that after years of dealing with "The Bullshit" and using alcohol as a way to "escape," was discovering that VR environments are uniquely effective for relaxation, meditation, and stress reduction, ultimately improving overall well-being and mental health. VR boosts productivity and helps you de-stress and unwind at the end of the Day—like alcohol without the hangover.

VR is an additive technology that expands your options rather than replacing them.

We will examine outdated practices and habits that no longer serve us in the modern work environment. Then, we will delve into the nuts and bolts of setting up your day for success using VR.

9

WHAT TO DO PART II

On a beautiful morning, the sun cast a golden glow on the steep rock face Alex had been preparing to climb for four months. Every hold, heel hook, and mantle had been meticulously studied, visualized, and committed to memory. Today was the day he would put all his preparation to the test.

As Alex reached the halfway point, he paused to chalk his free hand, soaking in the breathtaking view for just a second, with his knee jammed in a crevice. The vast landscape stretched out beneath him, magically filling him with a deep appreciation of both the natural beauty and the challenge of the climb. However, this morning, his preparation was a little rushed. He deliberately skipped a small step he had used since he started climbing seriously at about thirteen. He usually spent 8-10 minutes stretching his fingers, wrists, shoulders, back, and knees, in that order, always in that order. But today, because he promised to be home early the next day, he had to start shortly after he arrived at the mountain and didn't stretch his back and knees - he brushed it off as the new normal, gruffly telling himself, *"for God sakes I've been climbing for 20 years, what's the big deal"* and pushed on.

Yet, amidst the awe-inspiring scenery, the challenge of the mountain, and the warm feeling of flow, a seed of doubt began to sprout in Alex's mind. Was today the day, with a new wife and baby and blossoming career in climbing, when he now had a lot to lose... Did he have what it takes to handle the mountain and these new outside stresses?

As if responding to his momentary lapse, a strong gust of wind suddenly lifted his body, shifting his center of mass slightly. Just then, his fist, which was forced into a crevice (called a fist jam) for support, also shifted and ... shit...shit...shit... FUCK! He felt the instantaneous and unmistakable pull of gravity.

A split second later, his fist, still tightly clenched, was met by the walls of the crevice just inches below, and no more give - he would be fine. While it was only a 2-3 inch shift, a paralyzing jolt of electricity was discharged through his body, and 1 mg of pure epinephrine (adrenaline) was shot into his system. His heart rate spiked, shattering his tranquil flow state. For a fleeting yet eternal moment, sheer terror paralyzed him. What was a long period of controlled focus, was now pure chaos and fear.

However, milliseconds before his conscious brain experienced the slip, his adaptive contentious was on the job, taking a very specific set of actions before he could consciously react. Because of his twenty-plus years of training and preparation, Alex's unconscious mind retrieved a method of visualization and meditation, perfect for the job and one he had practiced many times to calm his mind.

So there he was, dangling off the side of a rock face hundreds of feet above the rugged mountain base. With his pulse still racing, he shut his eyes and drew in a deep, deliberate breath through his nose, counting slowly to five. Then, with focused calm, he released it in a steady, controlled exhalation through his mouth, extending the count to ten. The rhythm of his breath, 5 seconds in, and 10 seconds out, became a lifeline, anchoring him amidst the dizzying heights and the vast expanse below.

After four or five rounds, his breathing and mind settled down. The adrenaline seemed to dissipate rapidly, and he was no longer at the effect of the powerful hormone. Now, thanks to his training, he knew he had to move. He focused on his next hold—no more thinking, just committing and executing the next move with certainty. Two moves later, he was back in that wonderful flow state after skillfully navigating a tricky overhang to traverse a rock jutting out like a giant's nose.

Certainty is one of the most powerful triggers for entering a flow state. As a climber, Alex has mastered the art of breaking a climb into smaller chunks or pitches. The goal is to reduce the cognitive load and create smaller, less complex tasks, ones in which he had more certainty and, quite literally, focused on the task at hand. This method of breaking down a long, intricate climb into shorter, simpler segments elicits a higher degree of certainty, a crucial ingredient for achieving flow.

Start thinking about your Work in this way; break down complex tasks into smaller, more manageable, and less ambiguous ones, providing more certainty.

The Case for VR in Deep Work and Flow at Work.

500% increase in executive productivity when in a flow state![1] ... really... Even I, a massive VR enthusiast was skeptical—that's a big number, but the fact that it comes from McKinsey & Co., typically the smartest guys in the room (all kidding aside, these guys are impressive), means we need to talk about flow in any discussion about productivity and creating a whole new way to work.

It's hard to create a mental model and picture of what 500% this looks like. But, when contrasted with what is more typical—which is just showing up to "work" and winging it until the adrenaline rush takes hold—the difference is stark. If you see yourself in the "winging it" category, you'll find the research from McKinsey an interesting, perhaps an unsettling wake-up call. I would bet you my truck that if you have read up to this point in this book, you are probably considered a serious business person, so these next four sentences may sting a little. Because the research specifically states that most of us are actually only productive for 2.3 hours per day.

We spend more than 50% of our days duplicating Work from previous days. We're in meetings 30-40 hours per month, and we check emails 36 times per day.

Perhaps most persuasive of all is the statistic that says the average knowledge worker is interrupted every 11 minutes (and it takes up to 23 minutes to get back into focus after a disruption)[2].

Another ritual deeply seated in our mindset is that we must separate our Work from our home and go to a separate building or space where others are also working. However, McKinsey's research challenges this practice. They claim, backed up by real evidence, that rather than being a place where real Work can happen, the "modern workplace steals your attention and undermines your best intentions at every turn." Your attention and focus are your access points to the deep world and flow, and why this is important is that you get your best Work on inflow and deep Work - that data tells the story.

More on Flow

If you've read even a handful of business or productivity books in the past decade, you've likely come across the concept of *flow*. But if you can confidently pronounce the name of the researcher who pioneered it at the University of Chicago in the 1970s—Mihaly Csikszentmi-halyi—you deserve extra credit (and maybe a round of applause).

His groundbreaking work on flow, along with the wealth of research that followed, has not only defined the concept but also provided practical insights into achieving and sustaining it.

We've all experienced flow to some degree, like when you're playing your favorite game or a musical instrument. It is that optimal state where you're challenged, deeply focused, and lost in a sense of time-lessness and well-being, driven by deep intrinsic motivation.

Flow is more frequently related to sports or music because, tradition-ally, it hasn't been seen as a natural part of the work domain. But because of technology (and the knowledge of the use of technology) leapfrogging, as we discussed earlier, technology often emerges before its most crucial applications are fully realized.

In sports, heart rate monitors were initially used to track and optimize athletes' training intensity and recovery. Coaches and athletes used this technology to gauge their cardiovascular performance during workouts and competitions, helping them adjust training regimens for better performance.

Over time, the medical community recognized the potential of heart rate monitoring beyond sports. Today, heart rate monitors are integral in medical settings for diagnosing and managing various cardiovas-cular conditions. They provide essential data for assessing heart health, monitoring patients during surgeries, and even for continuous monitoring in ambulatory settings.

Similarly, it's taken time to migrate from sport to business and productivity, but virtual reality (VR) is now recognized as a powerful productivity enhancer. Research by the Flow Research Collective shows that VR can significantly boost productivity, creativity, and learning by fostering conditions conducive to flow. VR provides an immersive, distraction-free environment where users can engage deeply with tasks, enhancing overall performance.

An interesting study published in *Nature*, in Spotlight, August 24, 2023, found that VR technology provides a high level of authentic immersion, which can enhance productivity and engagement. The ability to create "life-like" simulated environments helps users maintain deep focus and achieve flow states, which are crucial for high productivity.

Virtual Reality

Here are some key researchers and their studies that demonstrate the link between increased productivity and the flow state using Virtual Reality (VR):

1. Jin, S.-A. A. (2011):

· Study: *I Feel Present. Therefore, I Experience Flow: A Structural Equation Modeling Approach to Flow and Presence in Video Games*

· Findings: This study examined the relationship between presence (the feeling of being in the virtual environment) and flow in VR gaming. It found that a strong sense of presence in VR significantly enhances the likelihood of experiencing flow, which in turn can lead to increased productivity in tasks performed within the virtual environment.

· Source: Journal of Broadcasting & Electronic Media

2. Harmat, L., de Manzano, O., Theorell, T., Högman, L., Fischer, H., Ullén, F. (2015):

· Study: *Physiological Correlates of the Flow Experience During Computer Game Playing*

· Findings: This research explored the physiological aspects of flow during VR gameplay and demonstrated that achieving flow can significantly enhance task performance and productivity by improving focus and reducing the perception of effort.

· Source: <u>International Journal of Psychophysiology</u>

3. Kim, G., Biocca, F. (2018):

· Study: *Immersion in Virtual Reality Can Increase Exercise Motivation and Physical Performance*

· Findings: This study found that immersion in VR can enhance motivation and performance in physical tasks by promoting a flow state. The immersive nature of VR helps users stay engaged and focused, leading to improved productivity in both physical and cognitive tasks.

· Source: <u>International Conference on Virtual, Augmented and Mixed Reality</u>

4. Gai, W., Lin, C., Yang, C., et al. (2017):

· Study: *Supporting Easy Physical-to-Virtual Creation of Mobile VR Maze Games: A New Genre.*

· Findings: This research highlighted how VR environments could support flow by providing interactive and engaging experiences that keep users motivated and focused, leading to higher productivity and better performance in tasks.

· Source: <u>Proceedings of the CHI Conference on Human Factors in Computing Systems</u>

These studies collectively underscore the potential of VR to facilitate flow states, which in turn can enhance productivity by improving focus, motivation, and task engagement. Researchers have shown that

VR environments can reduce cognitive load by providing immediate feedback and clear goals, maintaining an optimal challenge-skill balance for achieving flow states. This real-time interaction with virtual elements helps streamline complex tasks, making maintaining focus and creating certainty easier.

The claim of a 500% improvement in performance comes from extensive research done by Suzie Kranston and Scott Keller of McKinsey & Co. into the productivity of executives. The research mainly focuses on the concept of *flow state* and is reviewed in more detail in the end notes. However, in summary, all the research from those executives in a flow state found they are five times more productive than on average, which is where the 500% comes from.

Understanding that achieving peak performance using VR involves more than just strapping on a headset. As someone dedicated to producing outstanding Work, you—yes, you—recognize the importance of a solid foundation—habits, rituals, and routines, including comprehensive training and preparation.

For many years, flow-related experiences were considered mystical or spiritual phenomena. However, recently, psychologists have identified flow triggers and demonstrated that they can be reproduced in controlled laboratory settings. This shows that flow is not merely some other-worldly mystic plane but an actual, achievable state.

There is now a substantial body of work from respected universities and well-funded private institutions like the Flow Genome Project to support the claims made in this book. If you're interested in the science and psychological underpinnings of flow, I recommend reading Steven Kotler's Work, particularly *Mapping Cloud Nine*. Kotler writes with unparalleled enthusiasm and clarity about flow, continually pushing himself to learn more from personal experience as an accomplished skier and mountain biker. As the Director of the Flow Research Collective, he offers invaluable insights.

Achieving a flow state or even deep work is exponentially more productive than the chaos of "winging it" at the office, which is fueled by adrenaline and shallow work. During a typical 8-9 hour workday, you might look busy and feel busy, multitasking and handling surface-level tasks, but you accomplish very little.

A Whole New Way to Work = Less Time at Work

The ultimate goal is to spend less time "at work" and more time doing things that will enrich your body and your mind, like exercise, sleep, meditation, being in natural environments, and face-to-face time with the people who empower you. This approach reduces your work hours and ensures that when you do work, you are revitalized, have energy, and have a clear mind.

What to Do

Rituals and Routines:

Human beings, particularly those in the top 2-3% in their professions, didn't get there by their genetic codes alone and have done the work. In the hours and hours of tedium, they developed rituals and routines to help them develop their skills and, however weird, are essential to help them do a couple of things:

1. The routines help them attain the experience of control and mastery over themselves and the environment
2. Rituals, most importantly create certainty around the task at hand.

When watching Rafel Nadal, the Spanish tennis superstar, a few things stand out as you watch him play a match. The first is the *heavy* topspin he generates on his shots, particularly his forehand. On average, Nadal's forehand topspin can reach 3,500 revolutions per minute (RPM), that's nearly 60 per second! Grab a tennis ball, hold it in your hands, and think about that... this high rotational speed contributes to the dipping trajectory, the impact on the surface, and the high bounce of his shots, making them difficult for opponents to handle.

In comparison, a top 50 ATP (World-Class) player like the young Canadian Dennis Shapopalyov is said to have the most beautiful topspin backhand in the game, but this generates spin in the range of 2,400 to 2,800 RPM, or 40% less.

Having grown up playing on the clay courts of Spain, Nadal realized at an early age that topspin is particularly advantageous on this surface. His relentless topspin and high bounce wear down opponents both physically and mentally. The constant need to handle heavy, high-bouncing shots can be exhausting and demoralizing, leading to more mistakes and decreased overall performance. This combination of factors makes topspin a highly effective strategy on clay courts, giving players like Rafael Nadal a significant edge. His mastery of topspin alone allows him to dominate rallies, control the tempo of the match, and exploit the unique characteristics of the clay surface to his advantage, and his record bears this out: he is arguably the greatest clay court player in the history of tennis. Nadal has an outstanding record at the French Open (Roland Garros), winning the clay court tournament an incredible 14 times with an impressive record of 112 wins to 3 losses.

In total, Nadal has won over 60 clay court titles, with a win percentage on clay hovers around 92%, a figure unmatched by any other player in the Open Era.

But the meticulous care and positioning of his two water bottles may be the most interesting.

As Nadal steps onto the court, he walks with a purposeful stride, often accompanied by his characteristic butt tugs at his shorts and adjustments to his headband. This initial part of his routine helps him settle into his competitive mindset. Once he reaches his seat, he places his bag down and begins the ritualistic arrangement of his belongings.

Nadal carries two bottles of fluid, one containing water and the other an energy drink or electrolyte solution. These bottles play a central role in his pre-match preparation. Before the match begins, Nadal carefully positions these bottles beside his seat, ensuring they are placed in a specific order. The labels of the bottles must precisely face the baseline he will be playing from, and they must be perfectly aligned with a small gap between them.

This precise arrangement is not voodoo or crystals; these are intentional, strategic adaptive behaviors that modulate Nadal's cognitive and emotional responses and serve as a mental anchor, providing Nadal with a sense of control and certainty amidst the chaos of a high-stakes match. The bottles are always placed in the same spot, a ritual he follows religiously, which helps him maintain his focus and composure.

As he prepares for the match, Nadal sips from each bottle methodically, often taking small, deliberate sips rather than large gulps. This controlled intake of fluids ensures he stays hydrated without feeling bloated or uncomfortable during play. Drinking from the bottles is also part of his broader pre-match routine, which includes various other rituals such as toweling off, bouncing the ball a specific number of times before serving, and adjusting his attire.

During changeovers, Nadal returns to his bench and repeats the ritual of drinking from the two bottles. He ensures the bottles remain in their designated positions, replacing them exactly as before. This consistent behavior provides a sense of stability and routine, which is crucial for maintaining his mental edge throughout the match.

Nadal's meticulous routine with the two bottles of fluid might seem like a small detail, but it is emblematic of his overall approach to tennis. No matter how minor, every action is part of a larger strategy to maintain focus, manage his level of certainty and control, and stay physically and mentally prepared. This dedication to routine and attention to detail has become a hallmark of Nadal's game, contributing significantly to his success on the court.

As you design and map your day, take a moment to notice the rituals you've naturally adopted, like waking up at a set time, showering, getting dressed, and making the bed. These routines set the tone for your day, but adding one or two specific work rituals that get you into the zone is key. These intentional practices can lock in that sense of certainty and readiness as you kick off your workday.

In the next chapter, I've outlined some routines I highly recommend to help you stay mentally sharp, confident, and fully ready to bring your best self to the day!

10

8 HOURS? REALLY?

The 8-hour workday is credited to Robert Owen and was a well-intentioned idea designed to promote a balanced life with equal labor, recreation, and rest. It was a revolutionary shift for its time, aimed at improving the quality of life for workers. But as we rethink how we go to work today, it's worth asking whether this structure, though once innovative, has outlived its usefulness in today's fast-paced, ever-changing world.

This brings us to an important consideration: our natural tendency toward status quo bias. We're wired to stick with what feels familiar, even when it's not serving us well. This bias keeps us clinging to routines and practices—like the 8-hour workday—that may no longer be the best fit for how we live and work now.

Before we delve deeper, let's consider an inherent human tendency: status quo bias. We're naturally inclined to maintain things as they are because they feel comfortable and familiar. This bias keeps us anchored to our routines, even when not optimal. Often, we don't even realize how entrenched we are in these habits and how they shape our lives.

But I'd ask you to slow down before you jump on the adrenaline express and ride it till the end of the day - and consider that the structure of your day is entirely just a function of a set of rituals and habits passed down from father to son mother to daughter. If we look back to the so-called good old days - it is clear the powerful marketing efforts of 1950s Madison Avenue and Hollywood largely shaped them. These are the same geniuses who promoted cigarettes, margarine, and sun lamps as symbols of a desirable lifestyle. These habits and rituals were born out of our natural aversion to loss or the fear of missing out (FOMO) and the deep-seated desire to conform to social norms.

I've been plagued, as have you, with living in and through such periods in which there were a lot of useless, ineffective, unhealthy practices, habits, rituals, and policies that we've just tolerated. In my twilight years, I've written this book as an attempt to excavate the *Bullshit* and call it out for what it is *BULLSHIT*, and then offer a choice to push through it or create something new. Because, as it stands, these periods add up to a disproportionately large chunk of our lives. The good news is that our *life* does not have to be a continuum of days in which we have no choice but to endure and step around or in it.

I recall in my mid-teens trying to explain this epiphany to my mother; although I couldn't eloquently articulate my thoughts at that stage in my mental development, my best attempt sounded like, "No, Mom... I didn't do it because... it is useless, and ah... its bullshit..." and even though my Mom was incredibly cool, that attempt at calling out Bullshit - as - Bullshit didn't end well. Hopefully, the years have provided some depth to the insight and nuance in communication.

The pandemic also taught me another important lesson: the eight contiguous hour work day, much like the classroom structure discussed above, is just more of... you guessed it. Bullshit and not suitable for much.

To truly understand our present day, we must dig into the past, much like the excavation process in constructing a building. This excavation begins by gently sweeping and lightly scraping the surface. Just beneath, hidden centimeters away, lie the beliefs, habits, and truths of the past 200 years—an amalgamation near the surface.

Like the confluence of sand, clay, and rock that forms the dirt on which a building stands, the blend of these historical beliefs shapes the foundation of our current practices. However, without much deep thinking, many of the beliefs and habits from the 19th and 20th centuries no longer serve us today. Worse, they can be detrimental to our well-being and productivity.

Consider these examples that shatter outdated beliefs: In the early 20th century, society largely confined women to the home. Today, they not only vote but also serve as Surgeon Generals and run for president. And remember when the "ideal meal" consisted of red meat, fries, white bread, and sugary cereal three times a day? Our understanding has evolved—just as our thinking must.

8 Hours... Who Made You Boss?

To understand how we got to the 8-hour workday, we have to go back to the mid-1700s, the Industrial Revolution, when work hours were notoriously long, from 12 to 16 hours a day, six days a week. Conditions were often harsh and unsafe.

During this period, the labor force comprised men who were often tasked with the most physically demanding and dangerous. Women also played a significant role in the labor force, particularly in the textile industry. They were paid less than men and often worked in similarly difficult conditions. However, child labor comprised a significant part of the early industrial workforce. Children as young as five or six worked in factories, mines, and other industrial settings. Their small size allowed them to perform tasks in the tight spaces in the mines - but their significant advantage was they made much less than adults.

Ownes was not some idealistic liberal academic but a successful businessman. Starting as a ten-year-old, he apprenticed as a draper and a textile merchant in Stamford, Lincolnshire, the East Midlands of England.

In 1791, at 20, Owen moved to Manchester, then a growing industrial city, to manage a cotton mill, equivalent to moving to Silicon Valley and managing a tech company. After a few years, he and a group of investors/partners purchased a Mill called New Lanark. I didn't mention that he also married the boss's daughter (no judgment).

Owens courageously resisted what he saw as exploitation and injustice of the day. He saw business as a way to institute a better life and morality. He is credited with bringing about a significant shift in how businesses could operate, with a focus on worker welfare.

Interestingly, he also established the Institute for the Formation of Character, which provided education for children and adults and childcare facilities to support working mothers.

What Robert Owen did was courageous and admirable, and at the time, in 1700-1800, it was appropriate, but that was more than two hundred years ago ...people!

It's also insightful to note that comparing one year in 1700-1800 to one year in 2000 purely chronologically is deceptive because it ignores the qualitative differences in the rate and impact of change.

As we explore the transformative power of VR in revolutionizing work, it's essential to understand the broader context of technological innovation and, specifically, its influence on our perception of time. Enter Ray Kurzweil, a renowned futurist and inventor whose predictions about the convergence of human and machine intelligence are shaping the way we think about the future of work. He currently serves as a Director of Engineering at Google, focusing on machine intelligence and natural language processing. Kurzweil, an MIT grad, has over 20 honorary doctorates and a pile of accolades for his innovations in fields ranging from optical character recognition to speech synthesis. His work and predictions have positioned him as a key thought leader in discussing how technology will shape the way we will go to work.

Ray Kurzweil introduced the idea that our perception of time's passage is influenced by society's accelerating rate of technological change. As technology advances ever faster, it distorts our sense of time. While we know Earth still takes 365 days to orbit the sun, Kurzweil suggests that our perception of those days feels faster because of how quickly things around us are evolving. This might explain why sitting in traffic or waiting for an email to download can feel like an eternity—our brains are racing to keep up with the rapid changes, making the slow moments drag on even longer.

Let's take a moment to revisit Owen's influence. He championed the rule of three, advocating for an 8-8-8 split—a balanced, symmetrical approach to work, rest, and personal time. Who could resist the appeal of reduced work hours paired with symmetry and the promise of "so-called" balance? Owen's call for balance not only improved the quality of life for workers but also, to the surprise of many industrialists, boosted productivity. More importantly, this transformative shift in labor history, driven by visionary business leaders who challenged the status quo, proved beneficial for both worker performance and company success.

I firmly believe that embracing a new status quo—*A Whole New Way to Work*—will lead to equally remarkable results.

Foundations

Now, as we orient ourselves to creating a whole new way to work, let's continue with an engineering metaphor and consider building a twenty-story office tower starting with the amalgamations of materials on which it was built. Our new metaphoric sub-straight comprises the three emerging social trends introduced in Chapter 3 as the foundation. The first of these trends is rooted in social psychology and cognitive science, and it states that the adaptive unconscious, the once-hidden aspect of our subconscious, plays a leading role in our behavior and performance. This remarkable feature significantly alters our perceptions, judgments, and decisions that guide our daily lives. This can affect our mood, stress levels, and overall mental health. Even without the mountain of data, it's self-evident that being in a beautiful natural environment is better for one's mental health than gazing through a human assembly line of depressed faces in cubicles. But what is truly astounding is that the adaptive unconscious processes regulate our emotions, filtering or reinterpreting information to maintain emotional balance, all without our conscious awareness.

The second trend also comes from research in the social sciences and addresses the almost magical/medicinal influence of the natural environment; this trend looks at the content of the environment. This trend exploits nature's powerful and somehow magical power to improve our well-being and performance merely by looking at and being in nature. There is also solid science to back this body of work called biophilia.

Go to a casino, and remarkably you feel "a lot" like gambling... maybe even some hanky panky, - this is trend #1

But walk through a forest or open grassland for just 30 minutes, and your cortisol levels and blood pressure go down. Your body releases endorphins and serotonin, naturally elevating your mood and relieving anxiety. This is trend #2

The third social trend is the emerging new science of motivation and our understanding of the additional dials and triggers that can lead to this amazing thing called the flow state.

If you've ever struggled with motivation—as we all occasionally do—chances are you've tapped into the practices of intrinsic motivation, particularly those outlined by Self-Determination Theory (SDT)[1]. Developed by Edward Deci and Richard Ryan in the 1970s and 1980s, SDT has, until recently, become a cornerstone for understanding what truly drives us from within. After decades of experimenting with different motivational strategies, I've amassed a sizable toolkit. It's packed with goal-setting techniques, self-reflection, and mindfulness practices, along with more affirmations and visualizations than I can count. While no approach is flawless, SDT has stood the test of time, especially when compared to the earlier era dominated by B.F. Skinner's extrinsic motivation theories are famously illustrated through Pavlov's dog experiments.

Another significant change is in the way we look at motivation. It was thought to come to us *from* somewhere - either from inside us, intrinsic: or from outside, extrinsic - the carrot and stick.

And that super-successful people seem to wake up motivated. But Jeff Haden, author of *The Motivation Myth,* has the most reliable method, suggesting that you and I are the source of the most valuable and long-acting forms of motivation, and it is only through our hard work and progress that we become motivated, rather than waiting for motivation to inspire us to work.

However, if you're like I am, you will intuitively sense that true motivation comes from a little of both. As it happens, there has been a recent modification for personal motivation theory based on the research by Dr. Zach Davis, which focuses on the psychological and emotional aspects of both internal and extrinsic motivation found in his book *Appalachian Trials*.[2] The research demonstrated that intrinsic motivation may not be enough, and that extrinsic motivation, added the right way, can be a crucial ingredient to get through the finish line. So we will take this knowledge into designing your map.

Your MAP

With a solid understanding of the foundations for creating a new way to work, let's revisit the MAP metaphor from Chapter 3, which serves as our route to a more fulfilling and productive work life. While not perfect, the acronym MAP—Mastery, Autonomy, and Personal Connections/Purpose—effectively captures the key elements of this journey. It's important to note that while mastery, autonomy, and personal connection are triggers for a flow state, achieving flow daily can be challenging. However, even reaching a *microflow state*, a scaled-down version, significantly improves the traditional cubicle environment.

For me, the MAP acronym and metaphor are easy to get and remember, and to build the case for MAP, I have used the inspiring actual lives of the real Alex Honnold and another climbing legend, Alex Lowes, who together make up the fictional Alex in this book. Both these men are truly remarkable, not just because he is the very best at what he does, but because of the way they have navigated the hurdles from their difficult upbringing in unconventional families to overcoming learning disabilities and physical limitations.

However, it is Alex Honnold who has achieved some degree of fame and success, which you may recognize because of the award-winning documentary film called *Free Solo* in which he is featured. The movie follows him up the 3,000-foot sheer rock face of El Cap in Yosemite National Park.

The significance of this achievement lies in the fact that, before Alex Honnold's feat, climbing El Capitan required a team of experienced climbers using ropes and other equipment, taking around 4 days and requiring overnight rests while hanging from the cliff. Alex Honnold, however, climbed El Capitan solo without ropes or a team, completing the ascent in just 3 hours and 56 minutes. As Steven Kolter says, that's like running a four-minute mile in under a minute. Here is a guy unconstrained by the current climbing culture, routines, and beliefs; he has discovered a whole new way to climb.

The Data

Imagine a day that isn't a copy-paste of your past routines or reminiscent of the rigid schedules from your school days. I'm offering a revolutionary way to work and live, one that breaks free from the *ropes* of the past and lets you design a new life, starting with how you structure your day.

Revolutionizing the way we work isn't a mere indulgence but a necessity. The truth is we have been forcing ourselves into a mold based on a system designed for a different era and a different kind of work. It's time to break free from this outdated system and create a workday that harmonizes with our natural productivity cycles and the demands of our current work environment, which is increasingly driven by technology.

A Whole New Way to Work is more than an appealing catchphrase; it's a blueprint for a healthier, more productive, and more satisfying professional life.

You should not merely work more or less. If you're like me and love to work, chasing the flow state. Instead, VR can help you get more quality work done in less time, giving you more quality free time and adding a new dimension of peace and satisfaction akin to actually being in Mother Nature.

Many of us who went through traditional public or private schools were subjected to a "war-time" assembly line design, moving from station to station, class to class. This method, efficient for World War II, was pure Bullshit for about 70% of us, but we had no choice.

The perspective shifts as we bring employment into the mix. Have you ever found yourself wondering just how much of your 8-hour workday actually entails productive work? If so, you might find solace in knowing that this isn't just happening to you.

In fact, the data alone tell the story and show that the most popular non-productive activities among employees include reading news websites (65 minutes), checking social media (44 minutes), discussing non-work-related topics with colleagues (40 minutes), job hunting (26 minutes), smoke/vape breaks (23 minutes), making personal calls (18 minutes), whipping up hot drinks (17 minutes), texting or instant messaging (14 minutes), snacking (8 minutes), and cooking in the office (7 minutes).[3]

There's a silver lining to this, especially if you're a freelancer or someone who works from home. While it might feel like you're not doing enough because you're not physically in an office, the research indicates otherwise.

If you're productive for merely three hours a day, you're matching the output of someone who spends eight hours in the office.

It was these slow-cooked revelations that led to the premise of this book. What if we really absorbed this data and merged it with upcoming trends? Rather than sticking to the traditional 8-hour work-day, we could, theoretically, trim it or even adjust our working hours to be from 11 am to 3 pm, or even 6 am to 10 am. The benefits would be extensive - we'd be well-rested, more focused, and even more productive. Now that's a workday model worth contemplating.

The Structure of Your Day - Your Way

Your day revolves around three core areas of focus:

Area of Focus #1 - Work

Area of Focus #2 - Relationships

Area of Focus #3 - Collaboration

The 3-D Diagram tells the story.[4] Each area is tailored by you to maximize your potential and satisfaction in aspects of your life that matter. There's no "best" allocation of time; instead, trial and error combined with research suggest that chunks of time starting at 60-90 minutes early in the day and 25-45 minutes later are most effective, aligning with how your body and mind function.

However, I personally allocate more VR time to work and collaboration and more in-person face-to-face time to "Relationships."

Your Journey

You have heard this for years, but now try it on for size...every journey to greatness, yours included, starts with a single step, a spark of curiosity, and an innate desire to chase the flow state and the ordinary.

Our castles are built on foundations of ambition, resilience, and a quest for fulfillment. But what if we could transcend the barriers of the physical world, and use Virtual Reality (VR) to not just envision, but genuinely enhance our performance, satisfaction, and success? In the realm of this progressive technology, the boundaries between the tangible and virtual blur, granting us an immersive experience unlike any other.

It's like a secret key, unlocking doors to unseen lands, where mastery isn't just conceived but consistently honed. Just as the great achievers in history have demonstrated, excellence is a product of disciplined routines and mindful rituals. Imagine a world where the consistency of these practices is exciting and not mundane, where adaptability is not a struggle but an adventurous exploration.

That is what VR offers—a world where our daily routines evolve beyond conventional boundaries. This stimulating technology immerses you in scenarios that expand your horizons, allowing you to practice and perfect your craft in a diverse, dynamic environment. It's like being in the shoes of the masters you admire, experiencing their journey first-hand, and learning in a way that traditional methods can't offer. VR can also be an excellent tool for mindfulness.

Picture the serenity of meditating on a peaceful beach or practicing yoga amidst towering mountains, all from the comfort of your home. It's not just about the physical, but also about creating a mental and emotional framework that supports success. The beauty of VR lies in its adaptability. As our goals evolve, so can our virtual scenarios, ensuring we remain on the path of constant learning and growth.

It's about beginning small, with manageable changes. Then, as we grow comfortable, we introduce more complex scenarios to test and push our boundaries to new extremes. It's about immersing ourselves in an experience that challenges us, encourages us, and ultimately transforms us. With VR, we aren't just observers or spectators of our growth, as we are when we watch TV, but active participants shaping our journey to an amazing life.

By using VR to improve our performance and satisfaction, we are not just adopting new technology but a whole new way of life—a life that embodies the wisdom of the masters, the discipline of routines, and the thrill of the extraordinary. So, let's step into this world of endless possibilities and manifest an amazing life, a life we truly deserve.

Ready, Set, Go!

As you know from the last chapter, rituals are crucial for high performance, and I have found them particularly important in the morning to help me "get my mind right."

Like Nadal, using rituals daily helps to gain certainty over our mind's chaotic environment.

Deep Work Preparation Rituals - Before Each Session

Ritual 1 - Ready: Comfort and Quiet:

1. **Find a comfortable spot**: Choose a consistent, quiet place to work. This helps reduce cognitive load and creates a positive, productive association with that spot.
2. **Avoid public places**: Avoid interruptions by avoiding coffee shops and parks.
3. **Prepare your drinks**: Have coffee or water ready, but avoid snacks to prevent distractions.
4. **Silence your phone**: Set a notice on your email indicating your availability times for the day.

Ritual 2 - Set ("Mind-Set"):

1. **Get your equipment ready**: Log in and set up your computer and headset. Test everything before starting.
2. **Review your goals and tasks**: Use an app like Notion for OKRs and day-to-day tasks, transferring the most important ones to today's list.
3. **Morning Mind: The Top Three**:

1: Gratitude:

- **Be grateful for what I have**: Start each day by reflecting on what you are thankful for. This sets a positive tone and helps you focus on the good aspects of your life.
- **Write down three things you're grateful for**: This simple act can shift your mindset and boost your mood.

2: Patience:

- **Be patient; good things come to those who wait**

"For still the vision awaits its appointed time; it hastens to the end—it will not lie. If it seems slow, wait for it; it will surely come; it will not delay." - Habakkuk 2:3

"A jug fills drop by drop." - Buddha

"It does not matter how slowly you go as long as you do not stop." - Confucius

"By your patience possess your souls." - Jesus (Luke 21:19)

"And be patient, for indeed, Allah does not allow to be lost the reward of those who do good." - Allah (Quran 11:115)

3: Living in the Present:

- **Don't project the good or the bad into the future; just take it step by step, one day at a time**. Focus on the present moment. Avoid getting caught up in future worries or expectations.

"Do not dwell in the past, do not dream of the future, concentrate the mind on the present moment." - Buddha

"The superior man is always calm and at ease, while the inferior man is always anxious and full of worries." - Confucius

"Therefore do not worry about tomorrow, for tomorrow will worry about itself. Each day has enough trouble of its own." - Jesus (Matthew 6:34)

"And do not walk upon the earth exultantly. Indeed, you will never tear the earth [apart], and you will never reach the mountains in height." - (Quran 17:37)

These teachings from various spiritual leaders emphasize the importance of focusing on the present moment and taking life one step at a time.

Ritual 3 - Go! Immerse and Execute:

1. Strap on your Quest 3 headset. Ensure it fits properly and is within Bluetooth range. Keep it plugged in when not in use.
2. Use the Immersed app by Meta to select your VR workspace. Choose environments that suit your mood.
3. **Experience a Shift:** Notice the change in your breathing patterns and focus within minutes of starting. This helps you "drop into" the zone.
4. **Understand Your Energy Profile**: Plan the length of your deep work sessions according to your energy levels. Start with longer sessions in the morning and adjust as needed throughout the day.
5. **Adapting Environments**: Choose virtual environments that enhance your productivity, especially during different weather conditions.

Plan your day with intention. Break up your day using good technology, like the Rize app, which reduces your cognitive load, helps you stick to manageable steps, and allows you to focus on one task at a time.

In Practice

Typically, this first session lasts 45-60 minutes, with a 10-minute break followed by a second 45-minute session.

After these deep work sessions, I take a break and return calls, read emails, and possibly attend a meeting - which I allow for on my schedule.

To apply deep work principles to working exclusively in virtual reality (VR) to accomplish more and work fewer hours, consider the following strategies:

The next step is to break down projects into smaller, very specific, and manageable tasks (or goals in the Rize vernacular) that you can tackle during one or a maximum of two deep work sessions. The Rise App prompts me to write a concise objective for a deep work session, and I can add a category and a tag.

Define a clear objective or goal for your work session, and take a few minutes to identify and write down what you want to accomplish and why it's important, but no need to obsess.

I use the Overview Tab and follow what Rize suggests to write down a goal, or you could call it an objective - using the OKR methodology.

This clarity will help you prioritize tasks and focus your efforts during deep work sessions. The Rize app provides me with a tool for session tracking and timing and a place to log and record my deep work.

Projects - using the Tagging Feature

Also, select a very useful category for analyzing your day, week, and month using the analytics.

Categories:

Categories are the three areas of focus, as discussed in Chapter 8. They help structure and manage different aspects of your activities.

- Work
- Relationships
- Collaboration

Tags

Tags are more specific labels that can be applied to goals within any category. They provide additional context or descriptors to help filter and find tasks more easily. Tags can be used to highlight particular attributes or actions related to the goals. Examples of tags might include:

1. Work - 100% VR

- Working on the business
- Working In the business
- Meetings

2. Relationships - 10% - VR

- Time with Family and friends

3. Collaboration - 90 % VR

- Exercise
- Gaming
- Meetings
- Shopping
- Art Galleries and Museums

Why Separate Categories and Tags?

Separating categories and tags allows for more nuanced organization and prioritization:

1. **Broader Organization with Categories**: Categories create a high-level structure, making managing different spheres of life easier and ensuring a balanced approach to goal setting and tracking.
2. **Detailed Filtering with Tags**: Tags provide a way to add multiple layers of specificity and context to each goal. This can be particularly useful for filtering and searching for tasks based on various attributes or actions required.
3. **Flexibility and Customization**: By using both categories and tags, users have more flexibility in how they organize their goals. For example, a goal related to a work project (category: Work) might also be tagged as urgent and long-term, allowing the user to quickly identify high-priority tasks requiring more time.
4. **Enhanced Productivity**: Combining categories and tags helps users to focus on the right tasks at the right time, improving productivity and ensuring that important goals are not overlooked.

The separation of categories and tags in the Rize app provides a structured yet flexible way to track and analyze your time. This helps you manage goals and organize your daily tasks in a way that suits your personal and professional needs.

Continuously iterate and refine your work, leveraging the focused attention of deep work to make meaningful progress.

While deep work is crucial for focused productivity, it also recognizes the value of exploring new ideas and gaining a broad understanding of VR technologies. Allocate time for both deep dives into specific projects and broader exploration to stay informed and innovative.

Using Your Energy Profile

Based on my energy profile, my high-energy periods are 4:15 a.m. to about 8 a.m. and 3-5 p.m. I take shorter breaks during these times but always move around. Adjust your routine based on your energy levels throughout the week.

How To - Breaks

Breaks are essential for maintaining stamina for multiple deep work sessions. Later in the day, as my energy wanes, it's also important to allow for recovery, walk outside, hydrate, breathe deeply, and relax my mind.

During breaks, I remove the headset and walk around. I will return calls and read emails. That way, I can walk around, ideally outside for 5-10 minutes, and catch up on the important emails.

Mental exhaustion

Frequent task-switching takes a toll on your brain, making you feel extremely tired. **Imagine it like running a marathon** – if you keep changing tasks, **it's like sprinting and then suddenly stopping** over and over again.

This constant switch depletes your mental energy, leaving you drained. Adapting to new situations or tasks feels overwhelming because **your brain needs to gear up** for something different.

Solid research[5] backs this up, showing that each switch between tasks uses up a significant amount of mental energy. It's like **your brain's fuel is running out faster because of all the changes**.

Understanding how these factors work together is crucial. Think of it as recognizing the connection between pushing your brain too hard and feeling mentally exhausted. The more you switch between tasks, the more you drain your mental resources, affecting your overall well-being.

How To - VR Meditations

There is plenty of good research that indicates the cognitive and health benefits of meditation, from increased attention span and focus to reduced anxiety and stress. Meditating in a VR space can actually enhance these benefits, transporting you to tranquil settings conducive to a deeper state of relaxation and mindfulness.

While deep work is crucial for focused productivity, it also recognizes the value of exploring new ideas and gaining a broad understanding of VR technologies. Allocate time for both deep dives into specific projects and broader exploration to stay informed and innovative.

Stop Multitasking... Just Stop

The pull of social media is much like the siren songs in *The Odyssey* —an irresistible force that lures us in, consuming our time and energy with endless scrolling and notifications. Instead of metaphorically lashing ourselves to our desks in a futile attempt to resist, we can turn to a more effective strategy: *substitution therapy*. This approach involves replacing social media distractions with something more engaging and productive, like using VR. For example, instead of mindlessly scrolling through feeds, we could immerse ourselves in a highly engaging VR environment that is engineered to keep us focused on deep work or relaxation. By substituting the siren call of social media with an activity that actually enhances our focus and well-being, we can break free from its grip and reclaim our time and energy. Like a muscle, our energy and focus can be exhausted over time.

Studies by the American Psychological Association show that productivity can drop by as much as 40% due to multitasking. An overwhelming 97.5% of people can't multitask effectively, and around 45% report reduced productivity during context switching. This constant shift not only increases stress levels and impairs decision-making but also results in a 15-point drop in IQ[6], equivalent to pulling an all-nighter. It's no wonder you're always exhausted.

11

WAKING UP TO A WHOLE NEW WAY OF WORKING

Six Seconds Ago

Alex's hands were wedged deep into the crevice, his knuckles pressing onto the rough, unyielding rock. His climbing shoes pressed into the surface, finding just enough friction to hold him steady. He exhaled slowly, then channeling all his energy, he freed one of his hands, muscled his body up and over... and nicely grabbed an easy rock. But the path ahead was daunting—the most treacherous part of the climb, a test of everything he had trained for. This wasn't just about reaching the summit; it was about proving to himself that he could rise above the challenges, both on the mountain and in life.

Five Seconds Ago

He saw the narrow slab he needed to cross—a razor-thin ledge, barely wide enough for a single toe. Beyond it, the holds were tiny, small pockets, large enough for a single finger. But he didn't hesitate. Years of experience and countless hours of practice had prepared him for this moment. With unwavering focus, Alex made his first move, trusting his instincts and his environment. He knew that the mountain was as much a part of his success as his own skill—the environment shaping his performance, just as it does in the workspace.

Four Seconds Ago

Doubt crept in. A sound, distant at first, grew louder—a voice, calling his name, disrupting his concentration. Who was shouting? Why here, in this place? Was it Sam? The thought tumbled through his mind, unraveling his focus. She was trying to compete and get into the spotlight, wasn't she? Always questioning him, holding him back, and distracting him at the most crucial moment. The thought took hold, shaking his resolve. If he could just get to the top, he would be OK. But just then, he turned his head for a second, but it was enough. His foot slipped, and the tiny holds beneath his fingers gave way. The grip he had on his goal, his career, and his life, weakened. No... this can't be happening... but it was inevitable, wasn't it?

Three Seconds Ago

Alex was falling, plummeting down the face of the mountain. His hands flailed, grasping desperately at the rock, but there was nothing to hold onto. Panic surged through him, cold and relentless. The mountain, which had once been his challenge and his source of strength, now became his undoing, dragging him down faster and faster. If only he could find something solid, something to stop his fall —but there was nothing. And Sam... what about Sam?

Two Seconds Ago

Time began to stretch and slow down. The world narrowed to a tunnel of blurred images and muted sounds. The fear that had gripped him moments before started to melt away, replaced by an eerie, almost peaceful calm. Visions flashed before him—his parents, standing in their warm, familiar home, the mountain always in view through his bedroom window. He could feel their pride, their unwavering love. Then, Mrs. Harper, his fourth-grade teacher, appeared, standing resolute between him and the bullies, her comforting smile reassuring him that everything would be alright. Finally, a breathtaking panorama unfolded before him—a vast, tranquil valley bathed in the golden light of the setting sun. The sight was so peaceful, so distant, yet it reached deep into his soul, soothing it. At that moment, he wondered if this was how it would end, a quiet resignation washing over him as he accepted his fate.

Just as the darkness began to close in, nature's healing, regenerative power offered him refuge. The image of his beautiful new daughter and the sound of his wife, Sam, lovingly calling his name, broke through the despair. It was a reminder that even in the most challenging moments, there is beauty, peace, and hope to be found.

One Second Ago

The sensation shifted—a gentle touch on his shoulder. The world suddenly stopped spinning, and the fall halted. He could hear her voice now, soft and familiar, cutting through the fog of the dream. "Alex... Alex, it's OK. It's just a bad dream. Everything's fine. You're OK."

He blinked, disoriented, as Sam's face came into focus beside him, her hand still resting reassuringly on his shoulder, grounding him back in reality.

The Dream and the Reality

As Alex woke from the dream, the intensity of the fall lingered in his mind, a stark reminder of the internal battles he'd faced throughout his journey. The dream wasn't just a nightmare; it was a reflection of the fears, doubts, and distractions that had threatened to pull him down—much like the outdated ways of learning and working that had once held him back. It was the environment, both physical and mental, that shaped his experience, just as the workspace shapes performance.

In the quiet aftermath, as he lay there, Alex couldn't help but reflect on what the dream had revealed. The fear of losing control, the doubt that had weakened his resolve, the distractions that had nearly cost him everything. Yet, amidst the chaos, there were moments of clarity —visions of love, support, and peace—that reminded him of what truly mattered. The dream had shown him that the climb, though treacherous, was not just about reaching the top. It was about trusting in himself, staying focused, and letting go of the things that no longer served him. It was about understanding that the environment plays a critical role in shaping outcomes—whether it's the literal mountain he climbs or the metaphorical mountains he faces in work and life.

Just as Alex had to trust in his abilities and focus on each move during his climb, the journey you've taken through this book has been about learning to navigate the complexities of modern work life. The lessons Alex faced on the mountain mirror those you've encountered here—letting go of old habits, embracing routines and practices, using new tools like VR, and doing the work to create your own motivation.

These are not just lessons; they are the keys to a more fulfilling and successful work life. Just as Alex realized that being in nature provided a deep, almost magical healing, you too can find that same peace and clarity in your own environment—whether that's on a real mountain or within the virtual landscapes you can now create. With VR, you no longer have to seek out the mountain; you can bring the mountain to you, shaping your environment to foster mastery, autonomy, and personal connection.

Moving Forward with Confidence

As Alex emerged from the dream, he realized that his fear was not something to be avoided but to be faced head-on. The fall wasn't the end; it was a reminder that even in the midst of doubt and uncertainty, he had the strength to find his footing and continue the climb. In the same way, you may face moments of doubt and fear in your own work life. But remember, like Alex, you have the tools and the mindset to regain control and continue your ascent.

This journey isn't about reaching a final destination; it's about embracing a whole new way of working as an ongoing process of growth and discovery. The peaceful valley Alex saw in his dream isn't just a vision—it's a symbol of the balance and fulfillment that is possible when you commit to this new path. By following the map of mastery, autonomy, and personal connections, you can create a flow in your work and life that leads to true success and happiness. The mountain is no longer a distant goal; it's within your reach, ready to be conquered on your terms.

A Future Full of Possibilities

As you move forward, equipped with the insights and tools from this book, picture yourself overcoming your own challenges with the same grace and determination that Alex found. The future is not just something to be endured but shaped by your own hands, using technology, habit, and practice. The lessons you've learned here are the beginning of a larger conversation about how to live with a whole new way of working.

Thank you for joining me on this journey. As you take your next steps, know that you have everything you need to create your own version of success and fulfillment. The climb ahead may be steep, but the view from the top is worth every moment. Welcome to a whole new way of working—your journey has just begun.

NOTES

Introduction

1. In *The Pleasure of Finding Things Out*, Richard Feynman reflects on the profound complexity of the universe, much of which exists beyond human perception. He describes standing at the seashore, marveling at the "rushing waves" and "mountains of molecules," a poetic reminder that what we perceive is only a fraction of reality. Feynman's insights illuminate the hidden richness of the natural world—electromagnetic waves, atomic interactions, and physical forces that shape our experiences but remain unseen.

   I chose to reference Feynman's reflections in this book because they exemplify the theme of looking beyond the surface, questioning assumptions, and embracing the unknown. His perspective encourages a deeper appreciation for the unseen forces that govern our world, a concept that resonates throughout this work. Feynman's ability to distill complex scientific ideas into vivid, accessible metaphors serves as an inspiration for exploring deeper truths in both science and philosophy.

   For a glimpse of his reflections, you can watch a version of this discussion here: Richard Feynman – The Beauty of Nature.

1. The Dawn of a New Era in Sales Engineering

1. Mornings shape the rhythm of the day. Instead of diving straight into emails, news, or the usual digital distractions, I choose to begin with something immersive and energizing—a journey through rolling countryside, a coastal trail, or even a futuristic cityscape. Thanks to HOLOFIT, I can experience these landscapes while getting in a solid workout from the comfort of my home.

   This practice is more than just exercise; it's about intentional engagement with the world. Throughout this book, we discuss the biophilic response—our innate connection to nature and how even virtual landscapes can reduce stress, enhance focus, and improve well-being. By starting my day with a HOLOFIT ride, I center myself, clear my mind, and create a sense of movement and adventure before tackling the challenges ahead.

   What sets HOLOFIT apart is that it makes fitness enjoyable. Unlike the monotony of staring at a wall on a stationary bike or forcing myself onto a treadmill, HOLOFIT transforms exercise into an experience—one that I actually look forward to. It's a reminder that technology, when used intentionally, can enrich our lives rather than just consume our attention.

   If you're seeking a way to start your day with energy, focus, and a sense of adventure, I highly recommend giving HOLOFIT a try.

[1] Getting Started with HOLOFIT

One of the best things about HOLOFIT is how easy it is to set up:

• **If your bike has FTMS Bluetooth**, you're all set! HOLOFIT will connect directly without any extra equipment. Some compatible models include **Body Bike, Star Trac, and TechnoGym recumbent bikes**.

• **If your bike doesn't have FTMS Bluetooth**, don't worry—you just need a **cadence sensor**. These small, affordable devices ($15-$5 **on Amazon**) track your pedal rotations and make non-Bluetooth bikes VR-ready. More on that after this section.

How It Works

Setting up a cadence sensor is simple: just attach it to your pedal, pair it with HOLOFIT via Bluetooth, and start riding. Your workout data syncs automatically, so you get a seamless, real-time experience. (see the next page)

Honestly, HOLOFIT has made indoor cycling something I actually **look forward to**, and something that totally takes me away from my daily concerns. I can't recommend it enough. If you're looking for a way to **stay motivated and make your workouts more exciting**, give it a shot! And if you need any recommendations, feel free to reach out—I'd be happy to help.

HOLOFIT by Holodia: Offers immersive VR cycling experiences compatible with various stationary bikes and VR headsets, transforming indoor workouts into engaging adventures. holodia.com

Other apps are as follows, but I have not yet tested them

VZfit by VirZOOM: Utilizes Google Street View to let users explore real-world locations virtually while cycling, compatible with multiple VR headsets. virzoom.com

Additional Accessories you will need with some of these apps :

Ocula VR Indoor Cycling Kit by Fit Immersion: Includes a Bluetooth cadence sensor and access to 360° virtual courses, enhancing the VR cycling experience. fitimmersion.com

By integrating these components, you can create a comprehensive and immersive virtual cycling setup that combines visual immersion with tactile feedback, enhancing your indoor exercise routine.

To purchase the HOLOFIT app, follow these steps:

1.   **Download the HOLOFIT App**: Visit the Meta Quest Store and download the HOLOFIT app to your compatible VR headset.

2.   **Choose a Subscription Plan**: HOLOFIT offers two subscription options:

  ◦ **Monthly Subscription**: $11.99 per month.

  ◦ **Yearly Subscription**: $83.99 per year.

Select your preferred plan within the app to gain full access to HOLOFIT's features, including monthly content updates and new workout modes.

myholofit.holodia.com

3.   **Ensure Equipment Compatibility**: HOLOFIT is compatible with various fitness machines:

○ **Rowing Machines**: Works with all rowing machines.

○ **Bikes and Ellipticals**: Compatible with all models when used with an additional cadence sensor.

I use an old and tired (broken-in) LifeFitness elliptical and a Peloton 2 and it works great.

For a list of tested devices and more details, refer to the HOLOFIT FAQ page.

4. **Utilize the Companion App**: Enhance your experience by downloading the free HOLOFIT Companion App, which allows you to track workouts, monitor progress, and connect with the HOLOFIT community.

The **FTMS Bluetooth**, Amazon – explain how to set it up and video.

2. In this book, we've explored **how technology can enhance, rather than distract from, our productivity and well-being**. One of the biggest challenges we face today is **managing our focus and energy**—especially in a world where digital distractions are everywhere. That's why I use and highly recommend **Rize**, an intelligent time-tracking and focus-management app that helps you **work smarter, not just harder**.

How Rize Works and Why It's Different

Unlike traditional time-tracking tools that simply log your activity, **Rize actively helps you improve your work habits in real-time**. It runs in the background on your computer, automatically categorizing your tasks and providing insights into how you spend your time.

Here's what makes it stand out:

• **Automatic & Smart Time Tracking** – Rize **automatically logs your time** without requiring manual input. It categorizes your work into different areas (email, meetings, deep work, distractions) so you get a **clear picture of where your time actually goes**.

• **Focus Session Management** – It encourages you to **work in focused blocks** using the **Pomodoro technique** or **custom deep-work sessions**. You'll get reminders to **take breaks at the right time**—helping you avoid burnout while staying productive.

• **Distraction Detection & Insights** – Rize helps you spot **where you get sidetracked**—whether it's too many meetings, endless emails, or unnecessary app-switching. Over time, you start seeing **patterns** that help you adjust and improve.

• **Work-Life Balance Tracking** – By analyzing your **active vs. passive work time**, Rize can help you see when you're overworking, when you need to take a break, and when you're actually productive versus just "busy."

How I Use Rize in My Daily Workflow

I've found that **Rize fits perfectly into an intentional work routine**, ensuring that I stay **productive without burning out**. Here's how I integrate it into my day:

1. **Start the Day with Clarity**

○ I open Rize in the morning to **review my past work patterns**. It shows how much deep work I got done, how much time I spent in meetings, and where I might have lost focus the previous day.

○ This helps me **plan my time intentionally**, scheduling deep-focus sessions for my most demanding tasks.

2. **Set Focus Blocks for Deep Work**

○ I use **Rize's Focus Mode** to structure my time in **90-minute deep-work sessions**, where I minimize distractions and tackle my most critical projects.

○ Rize tracks my **real engagement time**, ensuring I'm actually productive—not just sitting in front of my computer.

3. **Balance Meetings and Creative Work**

○ Meetings are unavoidable, but **Rize shows me exactly how much time I spend in them**.

○ If I see that meetings are eating up my focus time, I make adjustments—either **batching them into specific days** or reducing unnecessary ones.

4. **Reflect and Adjust at the End of the Day**

○ Before logging off, I check Rize's **daily summary** to see where my time went.

○ If I notice **too much time spent in reactive tasks (emails, messages, meetings)** and not enough on deep, meaningful work, I tweak my schedule for the next day.

Why Rize Aligns with This Book's Principles

Throughout this book, we've emphasized **intentional work, deep focus, and technology that enhances rather than interrupts productivity**. Rize embodies all of these principles.

• **It eliminates guesswork** – You get **hard data** on how you actually work, rather than relying on how you *think* you spent your time.

• **It helps you work smarter, not longer** – By identifying **when you're most productive**, it enables you to optimize your schedule for maximum efficiency.

• **It encourages balance** – Rize ensures that **rest and breaks** are as much a part of your workday as deep focus—helping prevent burnout and **promoting sustainable productivity**.

How to Get Started with Rize

1. **Download the App** – Visit Rize.io and install it on your computer.

2. **Let It Run Automatically** – No need to manually enter time; Rize **tracks and categorizes your work automatically**.

3. **Review Your Patterns** – After a few days, check your reports to see where your time is going.

4. **Optimize Your Workflow** – Use the insights to **schedule deep-focus sessions**, limit distractions, and create a **work routine that actually works for you**.

If you're serious about **enhancing focus, reducing distractions, and working more effectively, Rize is one of the best tools I've found**. Give it a try—you may be surprised at how much it transforms the way you work.

2. The Maps We Are Given

1. The Harmony Central website still exists, but its online community went under – while I used to to listen to classic rock and learn about the musician and equipment – I also found like-mined geeks sitting at home on the internet in the 1990's – there was no VR then just chat and audio.

   No single event "pulled the plug" on Harmony Central. Instead, due to evolving web habits, changes in management and site design, and fierce competition from newer platforms, its once-thriving community has diminished significantly over time.

2. The Immerse app and the Rize app are integral components of *A Whole New Way to Work*. Immerse offers a rich, interactive space that functions much like a "mental gym," enabling users to train their cognitive abilities, spark creativity, and experience profound moments of clarity—all from within a fully immersive digital setting. Its intuitive interface and extensive library of VR experiences make it accessible for both beginners and seasoned VR enthusiasts. To get started, simply download the Immerse app from your preferred VR platform (such as Oculus Store, SteamVR, or Apple's App Store), create an account, and explore the diverse virtual environments curated for mental and professional development. This tool not only enhances personal growth but also exemplifies the innovative, boundary-pushing approaches to work and well-being discussed throughout this book.

   In this book, we've explored **how technology can enhance, rather than distract from, our productivity and well-being**. One of the biggest challenges we face today is **managing our focus and energy**—especially in a world where digital distractions are everywhere. That's why I use and highly recommend **Rize**, an intelligent time-tracking and focus-management app that helps you **work smarter, not just harder**.

   How Rize Works and Why It's Different

   Unlike traditional time-tracking tools that simply log your activity, **Rize actively helps you improve your work habits in real-time**. It runs in the background on your computer, automatically categorizing your tasks and providing insights into how you spend your time.

   Here's what makes it stand out:

   • **Automatic & Smart Time Tracking** – Rize **automatically logs your time** without requiring manual input. It categorizes your work into different areas (email, meetings, deep work, distractions) so you get a **clear picture of where your time actually goes**.

   • **Focus Session Management** – It encourages you to **work in focused blocks** using the **Pomodoro technique** or **custom deep-work sessions**. You'll get reminders to **take breaks at the right time**—helping you avoid burnout while staying productive.

   • **Distraction Detection & Insights** – Rize helps you spot **where you get sidetracked**—whether it's too many meetings, endless emails, or unnecessary app-switching. Over time, you start seeing **patterns** that help you adjust and improve.

• **Work-Life Balance Tracking** – By analyzing your **active vs. passive work time**, Rize can help you see when you're overworking, when you need to take a break, and when you're actually productive versus just "busy."

How I Use Rize in My Daily Workflow

I've found that **Rize fits perfectly into an intentional work routine**, ensuring that I stay **productive without burning out**. Here's how I integrate it into my day:

1. **Start the Day with Clarity**

○ I open Rize in the morning to **review my past work patterns**. It shows how much deep work I got done, how much time I spent in meetings, and where I might have lost focus the previous day.

○ This helps me **plan my time intentionally**, scheduling deep-focus sessions for my most demanding tasks.

2. **Set Focus Blocks for Deep Work**

○ I use **Rize's Focus Mode** to structure my time in **90-minute deep-work sessions**, where I minimize distractions and tackle my most critical projects.

○ Rize tracks my **real engagement time**, ensuring I'm actually productive—not just sitting in front of my computer.

3. **Balance Meetings and Creative Work**

○ Meetings are unavoidable, but **Rize shows me exactly how much time I spend in them**.

○ If I see that meetings are eating up my focus time, I make adjustments—either **batching them into specific days** or reducing unnecessary ones.

4. **Reflect and Adjust at the End of the Day**

○ Before logging off, I check Rize's **daily summary** to see where my time went.

○ If I notice **too much time spent in reactive tasks (emails, messages, meetings)** and not enough on deep, meaningful work, I tweak my schedule for the next day.

Why Rize Aligns with This Book's Principles

Throughout this book, we've emphasized **intentional work, deep focus, and technology that enhances rather than interrupts productivity**. Rize embodies all of these principles.

• **It eliminates guesswork** – You get **hard data** on how you actually work, rather than relying on how you *think* you spent your time.

• **It helps you work smarter, not longer** – By identifying **when you're most productive**, it enables you to optimize your schedule for maximum efficiency.

• **It encourages balance** – Rize ensures that **rest and breaks** are as much a part of your workday as deep focus—helping prevent burnout and **promoting sustainable productivity**.

How to Get Started with Rize

1. Download the App – Visit Rize.io and install it on your computer.

2. Let It Run Automatically – No need to manually enter time; Rize **tracks and categorizes your work automatically**.

3. Review Your Patterns – After a few days, check your reports to see where your time is going.

4. Optimize Your Workflow – Use the insights to **schedule deep-focus sessions**, limit distractions, and create a **work routine that actually works for you**.

If you're serious about **enhancing focus, reducing distractions, and working more effectively**, **Rize is one of the best tools I've found**. Give it a try—you may be surprised at how much it transforms the way you work.

3. When the Rush Replaces Dreams

1. Lencioni, Patrick. *The Advantage: Why Organizational Health Trumps Everything Else in Business*. Jossey-Bass, 2012.

   Patrick Lencioni's *The Advantage* beautifully captures the adrenaline rush inherent in the struggle to impose order on chaos—a theme that has deeply informed my own journey and the legacy I witnessed in my father's footsteps. In this book, Lencioni articulates how the daily battle to wrest control from disorder can infuse our lives with a sense of self-importance and a focused, albeit short-term, purpose. This cycle of chaos and control, with its strange satisfaction and challenge, mirrors the personal experiences and energy that underpin *A Whole New Way to Work*. For readers navigating the complexities of modern work and seeking inspiration from familiar yet transformative struggles, Lencioni's work serves as an invaluable resource, reinforcing the idea that the fight against chaos is not only inevitable but also a powerful driver of growth and innovation.

2. Dante Alighieri, the renowned 14th-century Italian poet best known for *The Divine Comedy*, symbolizes a pivotal shift in perspective—much like the early innovation of eyeglasses in his native Italy. While Dante himself was not the literal inventor of eyeglasses, his era coincided with their emergence, which transformed the way people saw the world by providing newfound clarity and focus. This breakthrough is a powerful analogy for *A Whole New Way to Work*. Just as early eyeglasses opened up a clearer, sharper view of one's surroundings, the insights in this book invite readers to adopt a refreshed perspective on work and life. Both the innovation of clearer vision and the call for a new approach to work underscore the transformative impact of shifting how we see and engage with our challenges.

3. Epictetus is widely celebrated for his Stoic wisdom, and a popular aphorism attributed to him states: "If there is something in life you think you should be, then you should be that." Although translations vary, this sentiment encapsulates the Stoic imperative to align our actions with our highest ideals. For a classic reference, see Epictetus' *Enchiridion* (trans. Elizabeth Carter, Dover Publications, 2002). In *A Whole New Way to Work*, this principle underscores the call to transform our professional lives by embodying the qualities we aspire to. Just as Epictetus challenges us to live as our ideal selves, this book invites readers to

reimagine their work environment by actively becoming the person they believe they ought to be—turning vision into tangible, empowering action.

Expanding Human Potential Through VR and AR

Throughout this book, we've explored the ways technology can enhance—not replace—human intelligence. One of the most exciting frontiers in this space is **virtual and augmented reality (VR & AR), which are fundamentally changing how we learn, make decisions, and interact with the world around us**.

Stanford University's **Virtual Human Interaction Lab (VHIL)** is at the forefront of this research, providing compelling evidence that immersive technologies do far more than entertain—they **expand cognition, enhance communication, and reshape problem-solving in profound ways**. When used intentionally, VR and AR are **not just tools but cognitive amplifiers**, allowing us to **engage more deeply with information, develop richer insights, and collaborate more effectively**.

This aligns perfectly with the core idea we've discussed: **Technology works best when it augments human capabilities rather than attempting to replace them**. In the right hands, VR and AR are not distractions but **powerful extensions of our natural intelligence and creativity**. As these tools continue to evolve, so too will our ability to **learn faster, think bigger, and connect in ways we never imagined possible**.

I've pulled together a few key studies from VHIL that you might find fascinating:

1. Virtual Reality as a Research Tool

Authors: Portia Wang & Jeremy Bailenson

What It's About: This chapter explores **how VR helps researchers study human behavior** in ways that traditional methods simply can't. It's particularly interesting if you're curious about how **VR can simulate real-world scenarios to test communication, decision-making, and learning in a controlled yet immersive way**.

Read more: vhil.stanford.edu

2. A Looking Glass into a Research Wonderland

Authors: David Markowitz & Jeremy Bailenson

What It's About: This study takes a deep dive into **decades of VR research using natural language processing**. It highlights **how VR has evolved and why it's having such a profound impact on human behavior**. If you're someone who enjoys seeing **big-picture trends and data-driven insights**, this one is worth checking out.

Read more: vhil.stanford.edu

3. Multimodal Analytics in Virtual Reality

Authors: Tara Srirangarajan, Portia Wang, & Jeremy Bailenson

What It's About: This research looks at **how integrating different sensory inputs in VR (sight, sound, motion, and more) can enhance learning and interaction**. It's fascinating to think about how the right combination of sensory engagement can **deepen understanding and retention in ways traditional learning can't match**.

Read more: vhil.stanford.edu

Why This Matters

What I love about VHIL's work is that it **isn't just about technology— it's about the human experience**. Their research shows that when we **intentionally** use tools like VR and AR, we're not just playing with gadgets; **we're expanding our ability to think, learn, and connect in ways we never could before**.

If you're interested in diving deeper into their work, **I highly recommend exploring their research library**: **Stanford Virtual Human Interaction Lab**

The key takeaway? **The future of work, learning, and communication isn't about replacing human intelligence—it's about using technology to elevate it**.

Bailenson, J., & Wang, P. (n.d.). *Virtual reality as a research tool.* Stanford University Virtual Human Interaction Lab. Retrieved from https://vhil.stanford.edu/sites/g/files/sbiybj29011/files/media/file/virtual-reality-as-a-research-tool.pdf

Markowitz, D. M., & Bailenson, J. (n.d.). *A looking glass into a research wonderland: Decades of virtual reality scholarship explicated via natural language processing.* Stanford University Virtual Human Interaction Lab. Retrieved from https://vhil.stanford.edu/publications

Srirangarajan, T., Wang, P., & Bailenson, J. (n.d.). *Multimodal analytics in virtual reality.* Stanford University Virtual Human Interaction Lab. Retrieved from https://vhil.stanford.edu/publications

4. In *Life 3.0: Being Human in the Age of Artificial Intelligence*, Max Tegmark employs a powerful technology landscape metaphor to describe the evolving interplay between human intelligence and advanced technology. Tegmark conceptualizes life in three stages: Life 1.0, where both hardware and software are fixed by biological evolution; Life 2.0, where humans can alter their "software" (learn and adapt) while our physical "hardware" remains largely unchangeable; and Life 3.0, where both our hardware and software can be designed and reengineered. This vision paints a vast, dynamic terrain—a landscape of endless possibilities, challenges, and transformative opportunities driven by artificial intelligence.

This metaphor resonates strongly with the themes of *A Whole New Way to Work*. Just as Tegmark's depiction suggests that embracing technological innovation can fundamentally reshape human potential, this book argues that the future of work demands a radical rethinking of traditional models. In our new work paradigm, digital tools, immersive environments, and continuous learning enable us to redesign our professional lives much like Life 3.0 redefines our existence. Both narratives encourage us to navigate this ever-changing landscape with adaptability and visionary purpose, transforming challenges into opportunities for growth and empowerment.

Tegmark, Max. Life 3.0: Being Human in the Age of Artificial Intelligence. Alfred A. Knopf, 2017.

5. Herman Narula, co-founder and CEO of Improbable and author of *Virtual Society*, provides a compelling exploration of the benefits of virtual reality. In his work, Narula discusses how VR extends far beyond entertainment—acting as a "mental gym" that offers substantial mental and physiological advantages. By engaging with immersive virtual environments, individuals can stimulate cognitive resilience, enhance creativity, and rejuvenate their overall mental well-being. This concept of VR as a tool for mental fitness aligns with the transformative ideas presented in *A Whole New Way to Work*, further highlighting innovative approaches to personal and professional development.

6. At the heart of human motivation lies *Self-Determination Theory (SDT)*, a psychological framework developed by Edward Deci and Richard Ryan. SDT identifies three essential needs—autonomy, competence, and relatedness—as the forces that fuel our intrinsic drive to engage, persist, and ultimately thrive.

   I've chosen to introduce this concept early in the book because it illuminates why immersive technologies—particularly the Metaverse—are far more than just the next digital novelty. The Metaverse offers a depth of experience that speaks directly to our desire for freedom of choice, mastery, and genuine connection. Unlike traditional 2D interfaces, these virtual environments empower us to explore and create in ways that feel self-directed, fulfilling our need for autonomy. They invite us to hone new skills and face challenges that enhance our sense of competence, while the shared spaces and real-time interactions foster a sense of presence and belonging—meeting our need for relatedness.

   By weaving SDT into the conversation at this stage, I hope to underscore the Metaverse's human-centric potential. It's not merely about technology; it's about experiences that resonate with our deepest psychological needs, transforming how we learn, collaborate, and connect in an increasingly digital world.

7. Throughout history, human existence has been defined by labor. From the earliest hunter-gatherers to the industrial workforce, survival and progress were inseparable from physical toil. For centuries, technological advancements—from the plow to the steam engine—have gradually reshaped how we work, but never before have we stood on the brink of a transformation so profound.

   We are at the cusp of a shift unlike any before, one that moves us beyond the perpetual cycle of labor into a world where work is no longer the defining structure of our lives. The rise of automation, artificial intelligence, and immersive digital environments signals a transition from purely physical or routine cognitive tasks to a new era of creation, exploration, and self-directed purpose. The Metaverse is not just an extension of the internet; it represents a redefinition of engagement itself.

   This moment in history is about more than technology—it's about what it means to be human in a world where time and effort are no longer strictly tied to survival. As we navigate this transformation, we must ask: How will we use this newfound freedom? Will we passively consume, or will we embrace the opportunity to redefine work, learning, and connection? This book explores these questions at a pivotal moment when we are no longer bound by the constraints of

traditional labor but are instead stepping into a future shaped by creativity, autonomy, and meaning.

4. VR, the Safe Space

1. Alex Lowe, one of the greatest mountaineers of his time, once said:

   *"There are two kinds of climbers: those who climb because their heart sings
   when they're in the mountains, and all the rest."*

   Lowe's words capture the essence of intrinsic motivation—the idea that true
   passion comes from within, not from external validation or obligation. This quote
   resonates deeply with the themes explored in this book because it speaks to the
   fundamental difference between *doing something because we must* and *doing
   something because it fulfills us.*

   In the context of the Metaverse and the evolving digital landscape, this
   distinction is more relevant than ever. Just as climbers are drawn to the mountains
   out of love for the challenge and the experience, people engage with virtual
   worlds for reasons that go beyond utility—they seek connection, creativity, and
   meaning. The Metaverse, like the mountains, can be a place of exploration, self-
   discovery, and transformation, but only for those who approach it with genuine
   curiosity and intent.

   By including Lowe's words in this book, I try to highlight the importance of
   intrinsic motivation in shaping the way we interact with new technologies. The
   future will belong to those who engage with these innovations not just because
   they exist, but because they *make their hearts sing.*

2. The concept that individuals possess unique learning preferences has been a
   topic of extensive discussion in educational psychology. While many educators
   and learners believe in the existence of distinct learning styles—such as visual,
   auditory, reading/writing, and kinesthetic—empirical evidence supporting the
   effectiveness of tailoring instruction to these styles is limited.

   A comprehensive review by Pashler et al. (2008) critically examined the
   learning styles hypothesis and found insufficient evidence to justify incorporating
   learning styles assessments into general educational practices. Similarly, a study
   by Newton and Miah (2017) highlighted that, despite the widespread belief
   among educators in learning styles, there is a significant gap between this belief
   and the lack of empirical support for its efficacy.

   pmc.ncbi.nlm.nih.gov

   However, acknowledging individual differences in learning is crucial.
   Research indicates that factors such as prior knowledge, cognitive abilities, motivation, and personality traits significantly influence learning processes and
   outcomes. For instance, studies have shown that personality traits like conscien-
   tiousness and openness are associated with deeper learning approaches and
   better academic performance.

   en.wikipedia.org

   In the context of this book, which explores the integration of immersive technologies like the Metaverse into educational and professional settings, it's essen-

tial to consider these individual differences. While the traditional notion of learning styles may lack empirical support, the Metaverse offers diverse and customizable environments that can cater to various learning preferences and needs. By leveraging the flexibility of these technologies, we can create inclusive spaces that accommodate different learning strategies, thereby enhancing engagement and effectiveness.

Understanding and addressing the multifaceted nature of individual learning differences allows us to harness the full potential of emerging technologies, ensuring they serve as tools for personalized and meaningful learning experiences.

3. In *Strangers to Ourselves: Discovering the Adaptive Unconscious*, psychologist Timothy D. Wilson delves into the profound influence of the unconscious mind on our judgments, feelings, and behaviors. He posits that a significant portion of our mental processes operate outside conscious awareness, yet they critically shape our interactions with the world. This "adaptive unconscious" enables us to process information rapidly and efficiently, guiding our actions in ways we often don't realize.

hup.harvard.edu

Wilson's research underscores the substantial impact of environmental factors on our mental states. Our surroundings can subtly influence our emotions and behaviors without conscious recognition. For instance, environmental cues can affect consumer behavior, leading individuals to make choices they might not fully understand.

researchgate.net

In the context of this book, which explores the integration of immersive technologies like the Metaverse into daily life, Wilson's insights are particularly pertinent. The environments we inhabit—physical or virtual—play a crucial role in shaping our subconscious mind. As we transition into increasingly immersive digital spaces, understanding the adaptive unconscious becomes essential. By recognizing how virtual environments influence our thoughts and behaviors, we can design digital experiences that promote well-being, enhance learning, and foster positive social interactions.

Incorporating Wilson's findings into our exploration of the Metaverse allows us to appreciate the profound connection between environment and mind. It emphasizes the responsibility of creators and users alike to cultivate virtual spaces that not only engage the senses but also nurture the subconscious aspects of human experience.

5. The Impact of Our Environment

1. For Alex, the allure of this new environment was not just about novelty—it was about rediscovering a sense of autonomy and simplicity that had been lost in the noise of modern life. Like Henry David Thoreau's retreat to *Walden Pond* or John Muir's deep explorations of *Yosemite*, this space offered a refuge, a chance to

strip away unnecessary distractions and reconnect with something more fundamental.

Thoreau sought solitude and self-reliance, believing that by removing himself from the demands of society, he could better understand what truly mattered. Muir, on the other hand, found meaning in the vastness of nature, immersing himself in landscapes that reminded him of humanity's small yet significant place in the world. Alex's experience echoes both perspectives—longing for a retreat that wasn't about isolation, but about reclaiming control over time, attention, and experience.

This is why the virtual or immersive environment resonated so deeply. It wasn't an escape in the traditional sense; it was an intentional shift toward a life that felt more authentic, more self-directed. Just as *Walden Pond* and *Yosemite* became sanctuaries for those seeking meaning beyond the structured expectations of society, Alex saw this new frontier as a place to redefine work, creativity, and purpose on their own terms.

2. Philip K. Dick's *The Minority Report* offers a stark warning about the risks of predictive technology, depicting a world where algorithms determine fate, stripping individuals of free will and autonomy. In this dystopian vision, preemptive policing based on probability creates a system where people are punished not for what they have done, but for what they *might* do. This raises profound ethical concerns about surveillance, free will, and the potential for technology to become an instrument of control rather than empowerment.

I chose to reference *The Minority Report* in *A Whole New Way to Work* because it serves as a cautionary tale for the digital age we are rapidly entering. As artificial intelligence, the Metaverse, and immersive digital environments become more deeply integrated into our professional and social lives, we must be mindful of how these technologies shape decision-making and human agency. Just as the novel warns against a world where individuals become prisoners of predictive systems, today's real-world technologies—from algorithmic hiring tools to AI-driven behavioral tracking—pose similar risks if left unchecked.

3. In her extensive research, cultural anthropologist Natasha Dow Schüll of MIT delves into how meticulously engineered gambling environments can foster compulsive behaviors. Her seminal work, *Addiction by Design: Machine Gambling in Las Vegas*, reveals that the design of electronic gambling machines and casino settings is intentionally crafted to immerse players into a "zone" where time and space become irrelevant, leading to prolonged and often uncontrolled gambling sessions. Schüll's findings highlight that such compulsions are not solely a result of individual predispositions but are significantly influenced by external environmental factors—elements that can be consciously designed and modified.

news.mit.edu

This insight is particularly pertinent in the context of virtual reality (VR). As VR platforms evolve, developers wield considerable influence over user experiences through environmental design. By understanding the mechanisms that can lead to compulsive behaviors, as illustrated in Schüll's research, VR creators have the opportunity—and responsibility—to construct virtual spaces that promote positive engagement and well-being, mitigating potential risks associated with immersive digital environments.

4. Lanier's insights are particularly relevant to the themes explored in this book. As we navigate an era where digital platforms and immersive technologies like the Metaverse become integral to our daily lives and work environments, it's crucial to remain vigilant about how these tools shape our cognitive processes and behaviors. The design of virtual spaces and online platforms can either promote mindful engagement or contribute to passive consumption and automaticity.

By referencing Lanier's perspective, this book emphasizes the importance of intentional and conscious interaction with technology. It serves as a reminder that while digital innovations offer unprecedented opportunities for connection and creativity, they also carry the responsibility to design and use these tools in ways that enhance, rather than diminish, our critical faculties and autonomy.

For a deeper exploration of Lanier's views on reshaping our digital interactions, consider his TED Talk:

How we need to remake the internet | Jaron Lanier

6. The Roadmap To Leveraging AR and VR Technologies

1. **Revolutionizing Professional Development with VirtualSpeech**

In the past, mastering the art of public speaking, negotiation, or leadership conversations required either a dedicated mentor, an exceptionally patient spouse, or endless hours of trial and error in real-world situations. Few of us have access to a seasoned professional willing to provide consistent, honest feedback in a stress-free setting. Even with a mentor, the learning curve was often slow and dependent on the availability and willingness of another person to engage in repeated practice. *VirtualSpeech is* a groundbreaking AI-powered platform that transforms the way we develop soft skills, offering a new paradigm for professional growth that previously required human partners.

VirtualSpeech leverages artificial intelligence, virtual reality (VR), and real-time feedback to create immersive learning environments where professionals can practice critical workplace skills in a safe, judgment-free space. Whether it's delivering a high-stakes presentation, handling a difficult conversation with a team member, or refining negotiation techniques, this technology eliminates the need for roleplay partners and allows users to practice as often as needed.

What makes *VirtualSpeech* revolutionary is its ability to provide immediate, objective feedback—something even the most well-intentioned mentor or spouse struggles to do consistently. Using AI-driven analytics, the platform evaluates eye contact, speech pace, filler words, and vocal energy, offering data-driven insights that accelerate improvement. This means that instead of waiting for sporadic opportunities to practice with a real person, users can refine their skills continuously and systematically, developing confidence and mastery at an unprecedented rate.

The implications are enormous. Previously, skill-building required high-stakes practice—often in front of real audiences where failure had consequences. Now, *VirtualSpeech* enables professionals to rehearse and perfect their approach before stepping into the boardroom, client pitch, or job interview. This is not just a marginal improvement in training; it's a complete reimagining of how we develop and refine human communication.

In *A Whole New Way to Work*, I explore how emerging technologies like *VirtualSpeech* remove traditional barriers to growth, allowing us to cultivate skills once reserved for those with access to elite mentors or expensive training programs. The ability to self-train and receive AI-enhanced feedback is an unprecedented advantage, democratizing skill development in a way that was once unimaginable. We no longer need to rely on the patience of others—our best coach is now always available, ready to guide us toward mastery, on our own terms.

2. Esports apps are more than just a way to watch tournaments and play your favourite sport. They are fully interactive platforms that allow users to dive into extraordinary digital environments, where they can compete, learn, and even build professional identities. For millions of people, these apps are their gateway to high-stakes competitions, real-time strategy, and global community engagement—all from their phone, tablet, or VR headset. The numbers are staggering: by 2025, the global esports audience is projected to exceed 640 million, a mix of dedicated fans and casual viewers who are drawn in by the sheer accessibility and excitement of the space.

What makes esports apps so transformative is that they don't just simulate traditional competition; they redefine it. In the past, professional gaming was limited to those who had access to expensive setups, tournament invitations, and the right connections. Now, anyone with a smartphone or gaming rig can participate in leagues, train like the pros, and engage in real-time coaching and feedback. Think about your new typical Monday...where work and play seamlessly blend into immersive experiences that were once the stuff of science fiction. That's the reality esports applications are creating, and it's changing the way people engage—not just with games, but with competition, collaboration, and even careers.

Just like VirtualSpeech revolutionized skill-building for professionals, esports platforms create an environment where competitive gaming—and the work that supports it—can thrive in ways we never imagined.

Just like you no longer need a boardroom to develop leadership skills, you don't need a stadium to be part of a global competition. Esports applications create a "whole new way to work" by providing digital arenas where skills, strategy, and collaboration define success—whether you're competing, coaching, or creating content.

What's truly groundbreaking is the social and interactive nature of these platforms. You're no longer just a spectator; you're a participant in an environment that evolves around you. Esports isn't just a pastime—it's an entirely new space where the lines between entertainment, education, and work blur into something thrilling and full of possibility. This is the future, and it's happening now.

3. Edward O Wilsons Book, Biophilia 1984, In *Biophilia* (1984), Edward O. Wilson argues that humans are hardwired with an innate affinity for nature—a bond that shapes our emotions, creativity, and even cultural practices. I chose to reference this work in *A Whole New Way to Work* because it beautifully illustrates that our natural connection isn't just about environmental conservation, but is also key to enhancing our personal well-being and work performance. Just as Wilson suggests that reconnecting with nature nurtures our inner lives, my book explores how integrating elements of the natural world into our work environments can lead to more innovative, balanced, and fulfilling ways of working. By drawing on Wilson's insights, I emphasize that a truly progressive work culture recognizes and harnesses our inherent need for connection—ultimately paving the way for a healthier, more sustainable approach to work.

4. Research from top institutions provides compelling evidence that our environment can significantly elevate our moods. For example, a study out of MIT demonstrated that workspaces designed with natural elements—such as adaptive lighting, calming soundscapes, and biophilic visual cues—can improve occupants' emotional states, reduce stress, and enhance cognitive performance. In parallel, a comprehensive review from researchers at Harvard-affiliated institutions found that increased exposure to green spaces is consistently associated with improvements in mood, reductions in stress, and better overall mental health outcomes. Together, these studies suggest that integrating natural elements into our daily environments—from offices to urban neighborhoods—can play a vital role in boosting well-being.

    news.mit.edu

    pmc.ncbi.nlm.nih.gov

5. Attention Restoration Theory (ART) posits that our cognitive resources—particularly the capacity for directed attention—can be replenished by immersing ourselves in environments that naturally engage our senses without demanding focused mental effort. In simple terms, nature's "soft fascination," such as the gentle rustling of leaves or the flow of a stream, allows our minds to rest and recover from the constant demands of work and urban life.

    In *A Whole New Way to Work*, I argue that reimagining our work environments to include restorative natural elements is key to fostering creativity, reducing stress, and enhancing overall productivity. Virtual reality (VR) is emerging as a powerful tool in this context, enabling organizations to simulate immersive natural environments—even in settings where actual nature is scarce. By integrating VR experiences that transport employees to serene natural landscapes, we can evoke the same restorative benefits predicted by ART, helping to reset mental fatigue and improve focus during workdays.

    This approach not only transforms the workplace into a more supportive and healthy environment but also paves the way for innovative work practices that align with our inherent need for nature.

6. In *A Whole New Way to Work*, I draw on seminal research by Roger S. Ulrich from the University of Wisconsin to illustrate the tangible benefits of nature on human well-being. Ulrich's 1984 study, published in *Science*, demonstrated that hospital patients with a view of nature recovered faster, experienced less pain,

and had fewer complications than those whose rooms faced a brick wall. I use this research to make the case that the restorative power of natural environments is not confined to hospitals—it can be harnessed in the workplace as well. By integrating elements of nature, or even simulating them through virtual reality, we can create workspaces that help reset our attention, reduce stress, and boost overall productivity.

7. In this thought-provoking interview, Brian Greene and Jarod turn the spotlight on artificial intelligence by arguing that the true challenge isn't the technology itself but rather the human behaviors and decision-making that shape its development and application. Greene explains that while AI is advancing rapidly and holds transformative potential, its benefits or risks are entirely dependent on the intentions behind its use. He emphasizes that AI is merely a reflection of our values, and without proper ethical guidance and oversight, it could amplify the very human flaws we already struggle with—such as greed, shortsightedness, and a resistance to change.

Jarod builds on this by highlighting historical examples where human mismanagement and bias have led to unintended negative outcomes, suggesting that these same issues could jeopardize the promise of AI if left unchecked. The duo contends that instead of fearing a dystopian future ruled by machines, our focus should be on reforming our social and institutional frameworks. By addressing our collective shortcomings—through better education, robust governance, and ethical innovation—we can harness AI as a powerful tool for positive change rather than as a harbinger of disaster.

In *A Whole New Way to Work*, I use this conversation to underline a central idea: the environments we create, both physical and organizational, reflect our human nature. If we learn to design workspaces and technological ecosystems with ethical principles at their core—perhaps by leveraging tools like VR to simulate restorative environments—we can mitigate our own faults and pave the way for a more sustainable, humane future.

8. www.BRDorey.com/kayak

9. The most influential modern biography of Vincent van Gogh is widely considered to be "Van Gogh: The Life" by Steven Naifeh and Gregory White Smith, published in 2011.

10. Jeremy Bailenson's pioneering work in virtual reality (VR) at Stanford University's Virtual Human Interaction Lab has been instrumental in demonstrating the power of immersive virtual environments to shape human behavior, performance, and well-being. In his research, Bailenson has explored how VR can be used to enhance cognitive function, reduce stress, improve empathy, and even promote healthier behaviors. He utilizes experiential design in VR to offer real-time simulations that mimic real-world actions, allowing users to practice, experience, or perceive certain outcomes before they happen in physical reality. In *A Whole New Way to Work*, I discuss Bailenson's work because it highlights the transformative potential of VR in the workplace. His findings have been pivotal to my understanding of how VR can support mental health and performance. For instance, research showing how VR can alleviate psychological stress, enhance attention, and foster positive emotional states opened my eyes to the potential for

VR to rejuvenate the mind during the workday—much in the same way nature immersion does. Bailenson's exploration of how different immersive environments drive specific behavioral changes revealed insights into how VR can be used to craft tailored experiences that elevate mood, reset cognitive resources, and ultimately boost productivity. Reading Bailenson's work allowed me to bridge the gap between the potential of VR technology and the principles discussed in *Biophilia* and Attention Restoration Theory. By combining his research with these foundational ideas, I recognized how we can leverage VR in the workplace to combat mental fatigue, restore focus, and improve overall well-being, all of which are critical in shaping a more sustainable, innovative, and human-centered workspace. for 27 seconds

Jeremy Bailenson, founding director of Stanford's Virtual Human Interaction Lab, has been a pioneer in exploring how immersive virtual reality can transform human behavior and well-being. His work—most notably encapsulated in his book *Experience on Demand*—demonstrates that VR isn't just a flashy new technology but a tool capable of reshaping how we perceive ourselves, interact with others, and even perform our daily tasks.

Bailenson's research reveals several key phenomena relevant to rethinking work:

• **Presence and Immersion:** He shows that when people are immersed in a VR environment, they experience a heightened sense of "being there." This sense of presence can lead to real psychological and physiological changes, making VR a potent medium for inducing relaxation and reducing stress.

• **Embodiment and the Proteus Effect:** His studies illustrate that the characteristics of our avatars in virtual spaces can alter our behavior and self-perception. For example, when individuals adopt more confident or creative virtual personas, they tend to exhibit these traits in the real world. This effect has profound implications for workplace performance and self-efficacy.

• **Transformative Experiences:** Bailenson's work emphasizes that VR can evoke deep emotional and cognitive responses. By simulating natural or restorative environments, VR can help mitigate the mental fatigue of modern work, enhance creativity, and improve overall well-being.

In *A Whole New Way to Work*, I use Bailenson's findings to argue that our work environments can—and should—be reimagined. Just as a hospital room with a view of nature accelerates patient recovery, VR environments that incorporate elements of nature and supportive social interactions can boost productivity, reduce stress, and elevate mood in the workplace. Reading Bailenson's work was instrumental for me; it provided the empirical and theoretical foundation for understanding how virtual spaces can be strategically designed to improve performance and well-being, ultimately guiding my vision for a transformative, tech-enabled future of work.

7. The Power of Nature

1. In *The New Science of Everyday Awe*, psychologist Dacher Keltner (along with his colleagues) explores how moments of awe—those experiences when the ordinary is transformed by a sense of vastness and wonder—can fundamentally shift our perspectives and behavior. The paper reviews empirical studies showing that awe not only reduces stress and self-focus but also enhances creativity, promotes prosocial behavior, and improves overall well-being.

   In *A Whole New Way to Work*, I use Keltner's insights to underscore the value of integrating awe into our daily work experiences. His research provided a scientific framework for understanding how immersive, awe-inducing environments (such as those created through virtual reality) can revitalize our mental resources and transform work culture. By leveraging VR to simulate natural or other expansive experiences, we can create workspaces that elevate mood, stimulate creativity, and ultimately boost performance.

   Keltner's work is instrumental for my vision because it reinforces the idea that our environments profoundly impact our mental state—and that by intentionally designing spaces (virtual or physical) that evoke awe, we can foster a healthier, more innovative, and engaging way to work.

2. In their seminal paper, Dacher Keltner and Jonathan Haidt proposed that "awe" is a distinct, self-transcendent emotion triggered by encounters with stimuli that are vast—either physically, conceptually, or spiritually—and that challenge our existing mental frameworks. Their work explains that experiencing awe leads to a "small self," where our focus shifts away from personal concerns and toward a greater sense of connection and openness. This shift not only enhances creativity and cognitive flexibility but also promotes prosocial behavior and emotional well-being.

   In *A Whole New Way to Work*, I draw on Keltner and Haidt's insights to advocate for transforming work environments. By incorporating awe-inspiring elements—whether through natural settings or immersive VR experiences—we can design workplaces that help employees break free from mental fatigue, stimulate creative problem-solving, and foster a deeper sense of well-being. VR, in particular, allows us to simulate vast, awe-inducing experiences even in urban or constrained settings, aligning with the idea that evoking awe can reset our mental state and enhance performance.

3. Keltner and Haidt's research is instrumental to my work because it provides a scientific foundation for understanding how transformative experiences can reframe our perceptions and behaviors, making it possible to reimagine work environments as catalysts for innovation, collaboration, and holistic well-being.

8. The Crossroad

1. The phrase "turtles all the way down" has long served as a vivid metaphor for the problem of infinite regress in our explanations of reality. Its origins are rooted in anecdotal accounts—often told as a humorous yet profound story where someone

explains that the world rests on the back of a giant turtle, and when asked what that turtle stands on, the reply is "another turtle," and so on ad infinitum. This image, found in various philosophical and cultural traditions, encapsulates the idea that every explanation or system is built on layers upon layers of underlying assumptions.

In *A Whole New Way to Work*, I use this metaphor to highlight the layered complexity of our work environments. Just as the "turtles" represent an unending series of foundational supports, our workplaces are composed of interconnected layers—from the underlying values and organizational culture to the physical spaces and digital tools we use every day. Recognizing that there isn't a single "magic bullet" for creating a transformative work experience is essential. Instead, true innovation and well-being come from understanding and reimagining each foundational layer, whether through incorporating natural elements or leveraging virtual reality to create immersive, restorative experiences.

This metaphor has been instrumental in shaping my perspective: it reminds us that to build a whole new way to work, we must address every level of our environment, ensuring that each "turtle" supports a healthier, more productive, and more inspiring way of working.

2. Connect to a MacBook is only one method – also a windows or android OS work.
3. Visualize stepping into a serene space where your inner world aligns with your external task. You start with a challenge that's just right—not too easy to bore you, yet not too daunting to overwhelm. As you engage, you notice that:

 • **Time Dissolves:** Minutes or hours pass without notice because you're completely absorbed.

 • **Effort Feels Effortless:** Every action becomes intuitive; the task feels like a natural extension of who you are.

 • **Heightened Awareness:** Your senses sharpen; you become acutely aware of details while simultaneously feeling a profound sense of calm.

 • **Total Engagement:** Distractions fall away. Your mind is clear, focused only on the task at hand, allowing deep insights and creativity to surface.

Importance of Flow in the Book

The book centers on flow as a transformative force—a key to unlocking human potential. It argues that by deliberately structuring work and life to facilitate flow, individuals and organizations can:

 • **Maximize Productivity:** Instead of the fragmented attention that plagues modern work, flow offers a way to harness deep focus for creative and efficient output.

 • **Enhance Well-being:** Experiencing flow is not just about better work—it's also a pathway to personal fulfillment and happiness.

 • **Reimagine Work:** The book challenges traditional, rigid work structures. It promotes a paradigm shift where work environments and tasks are intentionally designed to trigger flow, thus fostering innovation and sustained engagement.

Creating a Whole New Way to Work

The basic idea is to rethink how we approach our work lives:

- **Designing for Flow:** Rather than imposing arbitrary deadlines or rigid schedules, work should be structured around tasks that align with one's skills and challenge level, making it easier to slip into flow.
- **Eliminating Distractions:** Modern workspaces are reimagined to minimize interruptions, thereby allowing sustained periods of deep focus.
- **Empowering Creativity:** When flow is encouraged, creativity thrives. Work becomes a dynamic interplay between individual passion and meaningful challenges.
- **Holistic Integration:** This new way of working is not merely about productivity; it's about creating environments where individuals feel motivated, energized, and fully alive—leading to breakthroughs in both personal and professional realms.

References

1. **Csikszentmihalyi, M. (1990).** *Flow: The Psychology of Optimal Experience.*

This seminal work lays the foundation for understanding flow, detailing its characteristics and its profound impact on creativity, productivity, and overall life satisfaction.

2. **Newport, C. (2016).** *Deep Work: Rules for Focused Success in a Distracted World.*

Newport explores how cultivating deep, undistracted focus—akin to flow—can transform our professional lives and lead to exceptional results.

3. **Kotler, S. & Wheal, J. (2017).** *Stealing Fire: How Silicon Valley, the Navy SEALs, and Maverick Scientists Are Revolutionizing the Way We Live and Work.*

This book examines how altered states of consciousness, including flow, are being harnessed by high performers to innovate and excel in various fields.

4. The flow state isn't limited to creative or athletic pursuits—it has broad and transformative applications across many professional fields. Here's how it can fundamentally enhance work in law, accounting, engineering, coding, and research:

Law

Lawyers often deal with intricate case details, voluminous documentation, and high-stakes decision-making. When immersed in a flow state, a legal professional can:

- **Rapidly Process Complex Information:** Absorb and synthesize large amounts of legal precedent and case law with clarity.
- **Enhance Persuasion and Argumentation:** Develop more compelling arguments as creative insights emerge seamlessly.
- **Improve Courtroom Agility:** Respond to unexpected developments with clarity and poise, thanks to deep concentration.

This heightened focus can lead to more precise and persuasive legal work.

Accounting

For accountants, especially during busy financial periods or audits, achieving flow means:

- **Minimizing Errors:** Deep concentration helps detect discrepancies in complex datasets.

• **Efficient Data Analysis:** Long stretches of uninterrupted work enable the rapid processing of financial information.

• **Enhanced Problem Solving:** When routine tasks are performed in a state of flow, accountants can also uncover innovative ways to streamline processes.

The result is not only higher accuracy but also improved productivity in an area where precision is paramount.

Engineering

Engineering tasks, which often blend creativity with analytical rigor, greatly benefit from flow:

• **Innovative Problem Solving:** Flow allows engineers to connect technical details with creative insights, facilitating breakthrough solutions.

• **Seamless Design Processes:** Deep focus enables the integration of complex systems and the iterative testing of prototypes.

• **Effective Troubleshooting:** A state of immersion helps engineers quickly identify and resolve system failures or design flaws.

This state of deep engagement is essential for both innovation and the reliable execution of engineering projects.

Coding

Programming and software development are perhaps the most vivid examples of work benefiting from flow:

• **Streamlined Debugging and Development:** Coders in flow can navigate intricate codebases with a fluid, almost intuitive understanding.

• **Enhanced Creativity in Problem Solving:** Innovative algorithms and novel solutions often emerge when developers are deeply immersed in their work.

• **Increased Efficiency:** Long, uninterrupted coding sessions can lead to cleaner, more efficient code with fewer errors.

The digital workspace, with its demand for precision and innovation, is tailor-made for the flow state.

Research

In research, whether in academia or applied sciences, the benefits of flow are profound:

• **Breakthrough Insights:** Researchers immersed in flow can draw connections between disparate pieces of data, leading to novel hypotheses.

• **Sustained Focus:** The deep concentration necessary for rigorous experimentation and data analysis is fostered by flow.

• **Creative Exploration:** Immersion in a task allows researchers to push the boundaries of conventional thinking, driving discovery and innovation.

Flow provides the mental clarity and sustained focus essential for advancing knowledge in complex and often interdisciplinary fields.

A New Paradigm for Work

Across these fields, the overarching benefit of flow is a reimagined approach to work—one that values deep, uninterrupted focus over fragmented attention. By designing work environments that facilitate flow, organizations can not only boost productivity but also foster creativity and well-being among their professionals.

References
- **Csikszentmihalyi, M. (1990).** *Flow: The Psychology of Optimal Experience.*

This foundational work describes the characteristics of flow and its transformative impact on performance and creativity.
- **Newport, C. (2016).** *Deep Work: Rules for Focused Success in a Distracted World.*

Newport's exploration of deep work provides practical insights into achieving flow in professional settings, emphasizing its role in productivity.
- **Kotler, S. & Wheal, J. (2017).** *Stealing Fire: How Silicon Valley, the Navy SEALs, and Maverick Scientists Are Revolutionizing the Way We Live and Work.*

This book highlights how altered states of consciousness, including flow, are leveraged across various high-performance fields to drive innovation and efficiency.

9. What to Do Part II

1. The McKinsey research on deep work and flow has become a touchstone for understanding how our modern work environment can be radically transformed. While the full technical report may not be available for public scrutiny in every detail, the study's widely circulated findings—most notably, that individuals working in a flow state can see productivity gains as high as 500%—offer compelling evidence that restructuring work to foster uninterrupted focus can yield extraordinary returns.

Below is a detailed look at the research and why it is central to the book's argument:

Detailed Insights from the McKinsey Research

1. Research Overview

The study investigated how work environments that minimize interruptions and promote deep concentration can fundamentally change productivity. McKinsey's analysis compared the output of individuals during typical, distraction-laden work sessions versus periods when they were immersed in tasks that allowed for a true flow state.
- **Key Finding:** Employees who could enter the flow state produced up to 500% more output than when their work was fragmented by constant interruptions.

2. Methodology and Metrics

McKinsey's research utilized a combination of quantitative and qualitative approaches:
- **Time-Tracking and Performance Metrics:** Workers' output was measured over various periods, noting the differences between focused work and distracted work.
- **Observational Studies:** Researchers observed work behaviors, noting

how quickly tasks were completed and the quality of the work produced during extended periods of focus.

• **Self-Reporting:** Employees provided insights on their perceived productivity and well-being when working without interruption.

• **Comparative Analysis:** The study compared industries and roles, demonstrating that even in fields not traditionally associated with creative "deep work" (like accounting or law), the benefits of a flow state were profound.

3. Interpretation of the 500% Productivity Increase

The 500% figure is not simply a numerical curiosity—it reflects the compound benefits of eliminating context-switching and the cognitive "cost" of interruptions:

• **Reduced Context Switching:** In a flow state, the mind stays locked on the task, which means that time lost to reorienting oneself is dramatically reduced.

• **Enhanced Cognitive Function:** Deep engagement sparks creativity and insight, allowing employees to solve complex problems more quickly.

• **Quality and Speed:** Not only does the quantity of output increase, but the quality of work also tends to be significantly higher. Tasks are executed with greater precision and innovation.

Why This Research is Central to the Book

Reimagining Work Itself

The study's findings serve as a quantitative backbone for the book's core thesis: that work shouldn't be measured solely by hours spent at a desk but by the meaningful output generated during periods of deep focus. This challenges traditional work models and advocates for:

• **Structural Changes:** Redesigning the work environment to reduce distractions—such as setting aside blocks of "no interruption" time, adopting digital minimalism practices, and rethinking meeting structures.

• **Cultural Shifts:** Encouraging a work culture that values deep concentration and recognizes the transformative impact of flow on creativity and productivity.

A Paradigm Shift in Organizational Strategy

• **Employee Well-Being:** The research shows that flow not only boosts productivity but also contributes to greater job satisfaction and lower stress levels, making a strong case for companies to invest in creating conditions for deep work.

• **Competitive Advantage:** Organizations that enable their workforce to enter a flow state are better positioned to innovate and adapt rapidly in a competitive market.

• **Evidence-Based Reform:** With a staggering 500% boost in productivity, the study provides empirical support for rethinking how we design jobs and workspaces. It underscores that a focus on quality and sustained engagement can fundamentally change outcomes across industries—from law and accounting to engineering, coding, and research.

Recited References

McKinsey & Company. (2012). *The Social Economy: Unlocking Value in the Age of Collaboration.*

This report lays the groundwork for understanding how structural changes in work environments—particularly those that facilitate flow—can lead to dramatic improvements in productivity.

In summary, the McKinsey study is central to the book because it quantifies the transformative potential of the flow state. By demonstrating that productivity can increase by as much as 500% when distractions are minimized, the research underpins the argument for a radical rethinking of work environments—one that prioritizes deep engagement, creativity, and well-being over traditional, fragmented work practices.

2. These data points tell a powerful story: in many modern workplaces, employees are spending significant chunks of their day on activities that, while natural, are not directly productive. Recognizing this breakdown is crucial because it highlights the potential gains from designing work environments that minimize such distractions. By curtailing non-productive activities, organizations could unlock more time for deep, focused work—which, as noted in related research, might boost overall productivity dramatically.

Recited References

· **DeskTime Research Studies:**

DeskTime's published findings on employee behavior have provided many of these insights. Their research is based on real-time tracking of thousands of workers and is frequently referenced in discussions about workplace productivity.

· **Harvard Business Review Articles:**

Multiple HBR articles have analyzed how fragmented workdays and non-work-related distractions affect overall productivity, offering further context and validation for these statistics.

· **RescueTime Insights:**

Similar data and analyses from RescueTime have corroborated the trends found by DeskTime, reinforcing the notion that non-productive activities take up a significant portion of the workday.

In summary, while the exact numbers can vary between studies and industries, the overall pattern is clear and credible: a substantial amount of work time is often consumed by non-productive activities. This insight is a key piece of evidence for advocating changes in how work is structured—aiming to reclaim lost time and enhance productivity by minimizing distractions.

10. 8 Hours? Really?

1. MAP—standing for Mastery, Autonomy, and Personal Connections—is a perfect metaphor for the book's central theme because it encapsulates the core principles of human motivation as defined by Self-Determination Theory (SDT) from Deci and Ryan. Here's why it works so well:

· **Mastery:** This element represents the drive to develop skills and achieve excellence. It ties directly to the concept of entering a flow state, where deep focus and practice lead to high performance and creativity.

- **Autonomy:** Autonomy emphasizes having control and freedom over one's work and decision-making processes. This not only boosts intrinsic motivation but also creates environments where individuals can tailor their tasks to their strengths, fostering greater innovation and satisfaction.

- **Personal Connections:** Human interaction and social support are essential for well-being and collaborative success. Strong personal connections enrich the workplace, providing emotional support and facilitating the exchange of ideas that drive progress.

Together, these three pillars form a comprehensive framework that reimagines work as a dynamic interplay of skill development, freedom, and meaningful relationships. This metaphor not only reflects the scientific insights from SDT but also offers a clear and memorable guide for designing work environments that enhance both productivity and personal fulfillment.

2. "In *A Whole New Way to Work*, the Appalachian Trail is presented not merely as a long-distance hike but as a transformative journey where every trial—whether a steep ascent, an unexpected setback, or the cumulative toll of physical exertion—serves as a catalyst for profound personal growth. The challenges along the trail are depicted not as mere obstacles to be overcome, but as powerful opportunities for self-discovery and the redefinition of one's limits. In a manner reminiscent of narratives like *Appalachian Trials*, this book argues that the very hardships which make the journey so demanding also spark an inner drive that fuels resilience and transforms struggle into lasting empowerment. Ultimately, this perspective deepens our understanding of why the trail captivates so many: it is a metaphor for the pursuit of a more meaningful, empowered self—a central theme throughout *A Whole New Way to Work*.

3. (EXPERT OPINION BY MELANIE CURTIN, WRITER, ACTIVIST @MELANIEBCURTINJUL 21, 2016)

4. www.BRDorey/3D-Venn

5. As we approach the final chapter—and with our publication date on the horizon for *A Whole New Way to Work*—it's essential to reflect on what modern cognitive research tells us about our work habits. Studies consistently show that frequent task switching isn't just an annoyance; it actively drains our mental resources. For example, research published in *PLOS ONE* by Hinss, Brock, and Roy (2024) illustrates that each time we switch between tasks, our brain undergoes a "reconfiguration" process that not only slows us down but also increases the risk of errors. In other words, every unnecessary interruption chips away at our productivity and leaves us feeling mentally exhausted.

This body of evidence supports the core message of our book. In today's hyper-connected work environment, the traditional model of multitasking is proving to be unsustainable—both for our efficiency and our overall well-being. As we stand at the end date of our current way of working, the research offers a compelling call to action: by embracing strategies such as time-blocking, monotasking, and deliberate breaks, we can reclaim our focus and energy. These methods not only help us perform better but also foster creativity and long-term job satisfaction.

6. Productivity and Multitasking

- **Up to a 40% Productivity Drop:**

The American Psychological Association (APA) and other researchers have documented that when we engage in multitasking—or more accurately, when we switch rapidly between tasks—our efficiency suffers dramatically. Each switch incurs a "switch cost," which is the time and mental energy required to reorient to a new task. Over the course of a workday, these small delays add up. Multiple studies (e.g., Monsell, 2003; Rogers & Monsell, 1995) have quantified these effects, showing that productivity can drop by as much as 40% when our work is constantly interrupted by context switching.

- **Why It Happens:**

Every time we interrupt a task, our cognitive system must retrieve the relevant task set and suppress the previous one. This reconfiguration process consumes precious cognitive resources that could otherwise be used to complete the task efficiently.

Multitasking Ineffectiveness

- **97.5% of People Can't Multitask Effectively:**

Surveys and experimental research indicate that nearly everyone—over 97% of individuals—is not truly capable of effective multitasking. Rather than handling tasks simultaneously, most people are simply switching between tasks, which degrades overall performance.

- **45% Report Reduced Productivity During Context Switching:**

In self-report surveys, about 45% of workers acknowledge that they feel less productive when forced to switch frequently between tasks. This subjective experience aligns with the objective data showing that switching costs dramatically hinder performance.

Cognitive and Behavioral Consequences

- **Increased Stress and Impaired Decision-Making:**

Constant context switching elevates stress levels by overloading our limited executive control resources. Research has shown that these interruptions can increase cortisol levels and impair our ability to make well-considered decisions. The brain's executive functions—critical for planning and impulse control—are taxed when we constantly shift gears.

- **A 15-Point Drop in IQ:**

Some studies and popular accounts have suggested that chronic multitasking can lead to a significant decline in measurable cognitive performance—often quoted as a drop of up to 15 IQ points. Although the exact figure may vary between studies, the underlying message is clear: the cumulative effect of constant distractions and task switching can degrade cognitive capacity. This drop is likely due to reduced working memory capacity and impaired executive function when the brain is perpetually overtaxed.

o For example, work by Ophir, Nass, and Wagner (2009) demonstrated that heavy media multitaskers scored significantly lower on tests of cognitive control and working memory compared to light multitaskers. While not a direct measure of IQ, these deficits are closely related to the cognitive processes that underpin intelligence.

Implications for Work

The research paints a compelling picture:

• **Constant Switching Drains Mental Energy:** Every interruption contributes to a significant cumulative loss of productivity and mental clarity.

• **Long-Term Cognitive Impact:** Over time, this constant switching not only increases daily stress but also impairs decision-making, which can have lasting effects on our cognitive performance.

• **The Need for Focused Work:** To mitigate these costs, experts recommend practices like time-blocking, monotasking, and creating distraction-free environments. By doing so, we preserve our cognitive resources, maintain higher productivity levels, and support long-term brain health.

ABOUT THE AUTHOR

Bruce R. Dorey, PhD, is a distinguished former Fortune 100 senior executive with over 30 years of consulting and operational experience. A visionary in workplace transformation, he now dedicates his expertise to speaking at events and coaching leaders and organizations to build high-performing, fulfilled teams in today's rapidly evolving work environment.

Bruce's innovative approach combines cutting-edge insights from flow state, cognitive science, and emerging AR/VR technologies to create environments where productivity and personal fulfillment thrive. Whether you're a CEO looking to reshape company culture, a manager aiming to boost team performance, or an individual striving to excel in the modern workplace, Bruce offers invaluable guidance for achieving success while maintaining balance.

Through his compelling books, transformative coaching sessions, and dynamic speaking engagements, Bruce empowers leaders and professionals to navigate the future of work with confidence, clarity, and purpose.

Creating Life Through Expert Coaching

The Craft of Coaching

Your life beyond 50 does not have to be predestined by the past; this could be the best time of your life!

All it takes is a new belief, a partnership, and a plan. Join Bruce for this exciting course that will show you step by step exactly what to do to become a successful coach and consultant in your field of expertise. Everything from beginner to ICF certification - The software, psychological assessments, OKR's, practice management and an amazing LinkedIn process to find your ideal clients.

Do what you love, and love doing it, all while generating a new stream of income you were unsure was possible.

Want more information?

https://brucerdorey-courses.thinkific.com/courses/the-craft-of-coaching-2022

ALSO BY BRUCE ROBERT DOREY, PHD

"Outstanding ... the first practical, original, and
science-based coaching book in decades—perfect for
coaching future leaders."

—Murtazali Dibirov MD, DBA
Managing Director, Swiss Leadership Academy

LIFT

THE NATURE & CRAFT
of
Expert
^COACHING

A fresh look at coaching in business

BRUCE R. DOREY

www.ingramcontent.com/pod-product-compliance
Lightning Source LLC
LaVergne TN
LVHW011327080426
835513LV00006B/236